More to Think About

THOUGHTS ON VITAL SUBJECTS

GEORGE M. RICKER, M. DIV., D.D.

(A SEQUEL TO *SOMETHING TO THINK ABOUT*)

NorTex Press

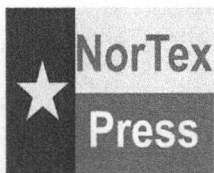

Copyright © 2011
By George M. Ricker
Published By NorTex Press
An Imprint of Wild Horse Media Group
P.O. Box 331779
Fort Worth, Texas 76163
1-817-344-7036
www.EakinPress.com
ALL RIGHTS RESERVED
1 2 3 4 5 6 7 8 9
ISBN-10: 1-935632-25-6
ISBN-13: 978-1-935632-25-2
Library of Congress Control Number 2011942401

To
All Progressive Christians
who have been able to accept
the biblical and theological scholarship
of the last two hundred years,
changing their beliefs accordingly,
and maintaining their faith
in the exemplary humanity
and God orientation
of
the Jew,
Jesus of Nazareth

Contents

Acknowledgments

What a myriad of people have had their role in the publication of this book! The authors in the bibliography have added their insights to my thinking and writing. The participants in my classes and seminars have, by their enthusiastic responses, encouraged me to organize my thoughts for publication. My one minute radio spots in Austin, Texas and newspaper columns in the *San Marcos Daily Record* gave me further impetus to publish.

In addition, my family has helped to complete the project. My wife, Frances, has not only been an essential encouraging factor, she also edited the manuscript and helped with the questions. Our son, Phil, expertly scanned material, organized the pages and put together the final manuscript. Our grandson, Philip, added expert typing in processing our corrections.

To all these I extend my gratitude. Without them this book would not exist.

Foreword

Over the last decade, there has been a remarkable resurgence of theological work which attempts to rethink and re-enliven Christianity. Writers from both ends of the spectrum, like Marcus Borg and Brian McLaren, have engaged in the quest for a Christianity that connects with a postmodern culture, yet does not lose the focus on faithfulness to the life and teaching of Jesus. Theologians like John Cobb and Philip Clayton have brought their prodigious intellectual gifts to tracing a new way of doing theology that moves beyond academic jargon to connect with the church and with real life.

Many pastors jumped into the dialogue and joined the vast movement of revitalized thought only to find that we were not the first ones aboard. George Ricker had taken a seat long before us, quietly working through sermons, newspaper columns, Sunday school classes and radio spots, seeking a mature faith that is authentic to the historic witness and also credible to the postmodern, even post-Christian world.

George is a marvel. At 89, he serves as Pastor Emeritus at University United Methodist Church in Austin, Texas, where I currently serve as Senior Pastor, and he continues to teach and write about the meaning of the Christian faith. I first became acquainted with George through his work at UUMC. Back in the 70s, he offered *Lifestyle Studies*, which featured serious reflection on the work of theologians such as Dietrich Bonhoeffer, Paul Tillich and Reinhold

Neibuhr. Ever the pastor, though, George's work always moved beyond theoretical issues to engage day-to-day realities. Long before much critical thought had been given to the full admission of gays and lesbians into the life of the church, George was there, speaking about the openness of the church to homosexual persons as an issue of justice. In the 80s, at the height of the arms race, even though the issue of nuclear disarmament was not popular, George lent his voice to the prophetic call for peace and for an end to the nuclear weapons.

Some might be tempted to pigeon-hole George as just another liberal theologian churning out mainline Protestant dogma. They will be surprised at the different ways he seeks to embrace and honor the opposite pole, even giving thanks, at one point, for religious extremism! The only kind of faith that comes in for harsh critique is one that is narrow and restrictive. And so while "progressive Christianity" may be the name that he favors, the faith that George outlines might better be described as a more expansive and inclusive Christianity. In approaching the issue of the interpretation of scripture, for example, he lifts up a view of the Bible that is "richer, fuller, deeper than it has ever been" thanks to the work of historical analysis and literary criticism. Similarly in writing about world religions, we're pushed not only to imagine the value in the diversity of religions but we're pressed to be personally shaped and transformed by the very different beliefs of others.

Particularly in light of the crisis North American Christianity now finds itself in with the growing decline in church membership and attendance, and the burgeoning numbers of those who are either uninterested or openly hostile to church, the practice of rethinking the meaning and the practice of faith is of paramount importance. Few will return to a church that simply repeats the well-worn formulas of days gone by. Undoubtedly some of what George Ricker says will not be popular. Good! The value of *More to Think About* lies in the summons to wrestle with the faith once given, not as a purely theoretical project, but as a movement of the soul toward a life of meaning and purpose that contributes to the transformation and healing of the world.

John Elford, D. Min.
Senior Pastor, University United Methodist Church
Austin, Texas

Introduction

Why a second volume on subjects to think about? For several years I did one-minute spots on Austin, Texas radio. This was followed by eight years of columns for the San Marcos Daily Record, San Marcos, Texas. My first volume, *Something to Think About*, published in 2007, involved a portion of the two enterprises. I arbitrarily used about half of the accumulated material. Since that volume was well received by individuals and a dozen or more Sunday School classes, I have taken the liberty of putting together volume two in the series. The chapters are multiple pages on the same subject. The miscellaneous chapter involves single pages on various subjects. In addition, I have added a chapter on reflections on the writings of my favorite author, Loren Eiseley, who died many years ago. His writings still communicate to our own time, and I feel an obligation to keep his work alive.

What right do I have to intrude into lives, homes, and churches the ideas that have come to me from years of reading and study? A few readers have taken issue with what I have written, but most of the pastors and laity of various denominations who have read my previous four volumes have been appreciative. They have recognized that most of my writing has been the result of contributions of modern scholarship which can be attributed to the Spirit of God working through communities of faith (progressive Christianity).

My radio and newspaper work proceeded from the conviction that the ideas expressed deserve to be part of public debate as sincere and honest convictions. This material has been gleaned from thinking and probing minds. Where people have found my words to be objectionable, I am sincerely sorry. For those who have been challenged or had their own thoughts clarified, I am grateful. Through the contributions of many, past and present, we are dealing with crucial issues of faith and life. Most of us struggle emotionally and intellectually with "the faith once given." I say welcome! The journey of faith continues and we are in a grand company that spans the ages.

GEORGE M. RICKER
Pastor Emeritus,
University United Methodist Church
Austin, Texas

CHAPTER 1

Thougths About The Bible

"Let's get back to the Bible," so I have heard said. The problem for me is that I do not see the Bible back there someplace. The Bible today is richer, fuller, deeper than it has ever been thanks to modern scholarship that involves linguistic study, historical analysis, and textual and literary criticism. The centrality of Scripture is today's Scripture correctly translated in modern idiom and faithfully interpreted utilizing the insights of a growing historical tradition.

The Bible today is better than it has ever been thanks to the discovery of thousands of manuscripts that were not available to earlier versions. And modern research into the history of that 1000 year period in which the Bible came into existence (from 631 B.C.E. to 367 C.E.) helps to differentiate what is historically relative (applicable to only one period in history) from that which is eternally relevant. What convoluted thinking occurs when this is not recognized!

Something to think about.

"God is the author of the Bible," so claim some biblical literalists. Be reasonable. Look at the facts. Almost 100 different authors are represented in the Bible and something of their own character is revealed in their writings. All of the authors were God-conscious individuals and were inspired (filled with the Spirit), but they wrote as human beings expressing their thoughts and ideas but revealing their own limitations and peculiarities. That much of their thoughts have universal application and validity is indeed one of the mysteries of this Book of Books.

Paul wrote, "See with what large letters I am writing to you with my own hand." Such words were added at times to his dictated letters. Did God write that? No, Paul was anxious to reveal that he was not completely incapacitated, though he may well have had an eyesight problem. Did God write the imprecatory Psalms where the Psalmist was railing out against his misfortunes, even questioning God? This would be God questioning God's self. Or all those poems of love and faith would be meaningless if God had written them to God's self. No, the Psalms are the outpouring of people who learned to bring before God their best and worst moments.

Human beings sensitive to the Spirit dimension of life wrote the biblical material. God's Word (Greek "logos") does not mean words but the disclosure of divine wisdom that comes through the experiences of God-sensitive people. To say that God authored the Bible is obscurantism at its best and overlooks the obvious evidence found in the Bible itself. Other examples are too numerous to mention in such a brief space.

We read the Bible for inspiration and enlightenment, for an understanding of the struggles of the people of God from Abraham through the early Christians. We read the Bible as a text book for a faith perspective on life and not because it was authored by God.

Something to think about.

Literalism as a method of biblical interpretation has been with us since the beginning of Christianity. Biblical inerrancy or biblical infallibility are more modern concepts not appearing until after the promulgation, by the Roman Catholic Church, of the infallibility of the Pope in 1870. Some Protestants were unnerved by that movement in Catholic doctrine. If the Pope is infallible when speaking from his chair of authority (ex cathedra), where is infallibility for Protestants? Some Protestants raised up a paper pope. As far as we know now, the first use of the word "inerrancy" was by Archibald Hodge shortly after 1870. Near the same time, Benjamin Warfield brought into usage the term "infallibility" in reference to the Bible.

Literalism, on the other hand, is of ancient origin, which does not make it necessarily absolute or right. Other methods of biblical interpretation are as ancient, the allegorical method being one. Perhaps one of the first literalists was Matthew. In his use of the Hebrew Bible as a predictive tool for the life of Jesus, he misused some texts. The most striking is his use of Zechariah 9:9 "Lo, your king comes to you; . . . humble and riding on an ass, on a colt the foal of an ass." Students of Hebrew know this to be Hebrew parallelism: saying the same thing twice using different words. Matthew took this quite literally so that in his Gospel he has the disciples securing two animals, putting garments on them and Jesus riding on two animals (Matt. 21:6-7). The other Gospel writers did not make this mistake.

All this is not to defame the Bible but to accent the fact that the authors were human beings with their own biases and shortcomings. The amazing thing is how the Word of God (God's creative wisdom) comes through the pages in spite of the humanity of the authors.

Something to think about.

I don't know about you, but I am always disturbed by articles that attempt to quote God: God says this and God says that. Such language is usually designed to support one's preconceived ideas. The attempt is to stifle debate and silence the opposition by an appeal to the ultimate authority.

In the use of the Bible we can say that Paul said, or Mark, or Isaiah, or the psalmist, etc.; but to quote God is an affront to dialogue. The Bible as the Word of God has nothing to do with the words being God's words. "Word" is the Greek translation of the Greek philosophical term "logos." The Word of God refers to divine, cosmic reason that creates and sustains the world. This cosmic wisdom is reflected in the Bible and its story of a people, but the specific words were chosen by God-conscious authors who were limited by their own historical circumstances.

The quoters of God have been found in error down through the centuries. What heinous crimes and inhuman acts have been justified by quoting God! Now is the time to stop this practice and engage in fruitful dialogue. God quotes along with private visions and theophanies are suspect.

Something to think about.

"One cannot believe the Bible ... and at the same time the theory of evolution," so creationists proclaim. Not true! I believe the Bible. I believe the Bible is the story of the people of God. I believe the Bible is God's Story, the story of God's search for a relationship with humanity. I believe the Bible is my story, an account of my people, giving me an identity that goes back almost 4,000 years. I believe that the Bible contains the Word of God, a creative wisdom (logos) reaching out for contact with humanity in a loving and reconciling way.

I believe in evolution as fact. The process is a theory not yet complete or fully developed but having developmental principles and a chronology that can not reasonably be doubted by any objective student of science. In fact, I know of no department of science in any major university that does not accept the principle of evolution. I believe in creation by process and not by fiat. I believe the universe came into being in the providence of God over an unimaginable period of time. But what is time to God? I believe that evolution has been rechanneled in a new direction in the development of mind and spirit.

I am a Christian. I believe the Bible for what it is: a book of many God-conscious authors with many types of literature. I believe in evolution as a fact.

The how of evolution is incomplete but essentially a correct theory of the process of creation. How about you?

Something to think about.

I am a Christian, I believe the Bible for what it is and for what it reveals. The Bible is not a book of science, economics, political philosophy or many other scholastic disciplines. The Bible is a book of faith not facts. Faith is revealed in the literature of poetry (Psalms), drama (Job), allegory (Jonah), parables (in Gospels), short stories (Ruth and Esther), essays (Ecclesiastes), letters (of Paul), apocalypticism (Revelation, etc.), mythology (Genesis 1-11, pre-history) and much more. All of these within an historical context of the development of the people of God.

At the same time, I believe in evolution as the best explanation presently available for the development of life from single to multiple cell organisms. To say that I cannot do this is an unwarranted presumption at its best and arrogant pride at its worst. I know there are Christians who do not believe what I believe, and they are, of course, free not to. I do not presume to say what others can or cannot do. I simply claim the right to judge the facts as I see them and to believe as I believe and to know in Whom I have believed and continue to believe in the midst of the knowledge explosion of the past hundred years. My faith remains secure because it is not dependent on the "facts" of science but on the Presence and Grace of that mystery we call God.

Something to think about.

Many make much of the Hebrew prophecies being ful-
filled in the life and ministry of Jesus. If this were true, this
would mean that Jesus made no decisions. He would simply have been a pawn going through the motions of fulfilling what
had been predetermined for him. A closed universe, predetermined, makes a mockery of human life. What would be true about
the humanity of Jesus would also be true about us. Omar
Khayyam, the Persian poet, expressed this fatalism:

"Tis all a Chequer-board of Nights and Days
Where Destiny with Men for Pieces plays:
Hither and thither moves, and mates, and slays,
And one by one back in the Closet lays."

Other possibilities present themselves. So called prophetic sections were used by the early Christian writers to tie the Hebrew
Scriptures to Jesus with their earnest conviction that he indeed was
the expected Messiah. In some cases Jesus himself patterned his
life after Hebrew texts (the suffering servant, riding into Jerusalem
on a donkey and not a more stately animal) in order to make a
statement about himself. The writers thereby took their cue from
Jesus' own self-identification with certain Hebrew texts. If we get
into the minds of early Christians and are not encumbered by contemporary standards, we can appreciate what they were trying to
do. This was not dishonesty or duplicity but being true to their
conviction that the Hebrew Scriptures prepared the way for the
coming of Jesus.

But, alas, some prefer the closed universe of magical prediction
than more rational explanations in spite of what this view does to
demean individual decision-making and personal responsibility.

Something to think about.

---

1. *Op Cit., page 35*

Conservative and liberal poles are evident in many aspects of life. James Davison Hunter's Culture Wars calls the poles orthodox and progressive. In the Christian Scriptures the orthodox are the Sadducees and the progressives are the Pharisees. How fascinating that Jesus had more in common with the latter than the former.

Biblical writers can also be characterized by these poles. The writer of Samuel was a conservative who insisted that God inspired David in much of his life (some incidents excepted, of course). In reporting on David's numbering the people (a census), the writer indicates that God moved David to do so (2 Samuel 24:1). The later writer of Chronicles writing about the same census (1 Chronicles 21:1) disagreed. He opined that Satan motivated David. Perhaps he noted, after the fact, that David used the census for a military conscription.

Biblical inerrantists (absolutists) have trouble with these texts. Was it God or Satan? Or was David's action a purely fallible human decision that was variously interpreted?

Conservatives then and now have been inordinately concerned about military matters. Liberals then and now tend to question excessive military measures.

Something to think about.

The patriarchy (male dominance) in the Bible is an accident of history and based on a primitive view of the relation between the sexes. Quoting the Bible as though every word came from the "mouth" of God fails to recognize the human limitations of the authors. The Word of God does not refer to the words but to the creative wisdom of God that is disclosed in the biblical message. This does not justify the institution of slavery, accepted by Paul, nor the understanding of the sexes current in biblical times. How significant that Jesus himself departed from the rigidities of his day in his relationship with women! Women could act like men as evidenced in the Mary and Martha story

Today, we are seeing the activity of God moving us toward an egalitarian relationship between the sexes. Yet the last gasp of patriarchy has yet to come. Some will insist on holding to the old patterns and justify them how they will. But many Christians and other humanitarians see the movement of the Spirit in history bringing us to a new day. Indeed the seer of Revelation "heard" rightly: "Behold, I make all things new." (Rev. 21.5)

Something to think about.

Some things in the Bible are historically relative, in relation to the concepts of heaven and hell for instance. The ancients used the words "ascended" and "descended." They were limited by their cosmology. To hold on to heaven being up and hell down is to be wrongfully tied to a cosmology that we know was primitive and inaccurate. For heaven and hell to be meaningful today involves some reimagining or reimaging. Many Christians are seeing heaven and hell not as places but as states of being.

One of the last century's most respected theologians, H. Richard Niebuhr, wrote about the confusion experienced by many Protestants today. In The Purpose of The Church and its Ministry, he notes that the confusion occurs, "when the Bible is so made the center of theological education that the book takes the place of God ..., and love of the book replaces devotion to the One who makes himself known with its aid." He continues with "identification of the Scriptures with God is an error, a denial of the content of the Scriptures themselves. To give final devotion to the book is to deny the final claim of God."

Is he downplaying the Bible, demeaning it in any way? Of course not! He asserts, "without the Bible, as without the Church, Christians do not exist and cannot carry on their work; but it is one thing to recognize the indispensability of those means, another thing to make means into ends." Christians who make the Scripture the object of their devotion and loyalty are guilty of centering faith in law (words) not the Spirit that moves in and through Scripture, nature and human relationships.

Something to think about.

QUESTIONS FOR THOUGHT AND DISCUSSION

1. What does it mean that parts of the Bible are historically relative?

2. Why are the words of the Bible not God's words?

3. What is the problem of literalism as an approach to biblical interpretation?

4. Are science and the Bible incompatible? Why or why not?

5. The Jesus story was told as fulfilling prophecy. Is there another explanation?

6. What is the difference between the Bible as a means or as an end (the last word)?

CHAPTER 2

Thoughts About Christians and Christianity

The kingdom of God is a rich but complex concept for most Christians. Basically it means the rule of God or the reign of righteousness. Obviously this has a future orientation since such a rule or reign is hardly recognizable in current affairs. Yet, the kingdom is very much present for those individuals or groups who try to live by it. As an inner reality, the kingdom lives within those who so attempt to orient their lives. When this happens definite changes occur that make life different. Think with me a moment about what the kingdom can mean to each of us.

To live by the kingdom of God leads me to ask not what I want but what is best for us: myself and others, my nation and other nations, my race and other races, my church and other churches and religions, my welfare and the welfare of all people. The kingdom of God embraces all of humanity and any restriction on our part is an offense against the One Who is the origin of the total human community.

Something to think about.

Christians speak much about the kingdom of God. The term is used in a variety of ways in the Christian Scriptures. I think we can say that the phrase is too rich to fit into one designation. Is the kingdom here, within, among, between, or yet to come? The answer is yes, all of these and more. But look with me at one thing Jesus said about the subject: "My kingdom is not of this world." (John 18:36) But the kingdom is in this world!

Jesus refused the messianic role of warrior-king. Apocalyptic Christians, like the Zealot Judas, are still trying to make him a warrior-king who will return soon to amass an army, destroy evil, and establish a kingdom. We can judge this matter by the life and ministry of Jesus who proclaimed that the kingdom is not of this world. It is not a political kingdom. The kingdom is in this world like leaven and the mustard seed, working slowly and deliberately to bring righteousness into the world. Not by coercion! Not by trying to make this a Christian nation by fiat! Not by trying to control the political process! The kingdom will come by compassionate and caring love, attempting to reconcile the poor, the sick, the destitute, and the marginalized by inclusion and not exclusion. Some would like to hasten the process by controlling the government; but in harmony with our long established principle of separation of church and state: Religious influence—Yes! Religious control—No!

Something to think about.

Christians vary in their opinions about other religions. Some hold the exclusivist position (that held by the most conservative Christians and fundamentalists) that salvation (whatever they mean by that term) is only through Jesus Christ. All outside are "lost." Different from the exclusivist, the inclusivist position rejects the concept that God condemns those outside of Christianity. For the inclusivists, many non-Christian traditions mediate the light of God and have saving functions. This position sees many others as anonymous Christians but lacking in the fullness of the faith. The pluralist position believes that all great religions mediate full salvation to believers by centering them in Ultimate Reality by whatever name it is called. For the pluralist what the name Jesus means is that God, Ultimate Reality, saves. So the pluralist affirms that we can learn something from others, that Christians do not have a monopoly on religious truth.

A fourth position is now emerging in the writings of a contemporary theologian, John B. Cobb, Jr., who writes about transformationism: changes made possible as we are open to the wisdom and goodness found in others.

Something to think about.

What are Christians to think of other religions? John Cobb, Jr. believes that Jews and Christians have, through the centuries, learned from other religions. Our heritage can only be fully understood in the light of what we have learned from others. He claims that such learning should not be confined to the past. I agree with him.

A study of Judaism reveals that Abraham brought with him the Epic of Creation and the ethical Code of Hammurabi from ancient Babylonia. Each of these is reflected in the Hebrew Scriptures. They also learned from the Egyptians and the monotheism of the Egyptian pharaoh Ikhnaton. Before Egypt the Jews were henotheists (holding to one God for them but recognizing the gods of others). They also borrowed from the Canaanites, the Persians, and the Greeks. The concepts of heaven and hell as "places" of rewards and punishments came from Persian Zoroastrianism; and the personification of Satan came from Shaitin, the god of evil in Zoroastrian theology. Before the exile, the Hebrew word "satan" was used to refer to any adversary. More could be said about Jewish religion absorbing from other traditions. And Christians have learned from others, but that waits for the next page.

Something to think about.

Have Christians learned from other philosophies and religions? The transformationist view of inter-religious relationships gives a resounding yes. The facts of history confirm such a view. The last page dealt with how the Jews learned and borrowed from others.

What about Christianity? Paul was well versed in Greek philosophy.

His writings show learning from stoicism. John's Gospel and Paul's letters reveal some borrowed language from gnostic redemption myths. Is Christianity today like that of the first centuries, the 14th century, the 17th, or the 19th? Obviously not! We have learned from the intellectual advancements of the centuries and have profited by our relationship with the philosophy and theology of other traditions. A great lack of faith is seen in the fear of being affected by wisdom from other sources. Faith in Jesus Christ encourages us to be open to others and to profit from the insights of others. Did not Jesus say that he has sheep that are not of this fold? And did God leave God's self without a witness in other cultures?

John Cobb holds that Christians look forward to a fullness of life that we do not now possess. We are in fact unusual among religions in that most others appear less open to learnings from others. Most traditions find completion in the past whereas Christians look ahead to the future. The Judeo-Christian view of history includes the concept of a journey of faith, that the fulfillment of history is not yet, that the kingdom of God is here only in a provisional sense. Of course, some Christians hold fast to past formulations and fear change, but this says more about the human desire for worldly security than it does about Christianity. But what about learning from differences within Christianity?

Something to think about.

As a mainline Christian I am encouraged by what is happening in our state and country. Wherever the Religious Right's agenda is made known, candidates are being defeated. Often the majority of Christians have had a hangdogged attitude about the reduction of members in their denominations. Mainliners need to be patient with history. Our standard-brand, historical, churches (with roots in hundreds to almost 2,000 years of existence) are more suited than the Religious Right to respond to the ongoing changes in society.

The process of adaptation and response has been successful. The effort of transvaluation (accepting the values inherent in old formulations but not being bound to the cosmology or thought-forms of the past) is continuing. Programs, education, missional outreach, and other services continue. Mainline congregations still flourish. Lives are being enriched. The Lord is being worshipped in creative ways. The majority of Christians are not rejecting the challenges of contemporary culture. They are very much in the world, responding to it, and bringing a transcendent perspective. History is not with the absolutists, those who refuse to change, or who try to live with certainties. Uncertainty is built into the universe which quantum physics is now demonstrating.

Something to think about.

Why are we so threatened by differences? Different ideas, different nationalities, and different races tend to place some people on edge. We want sameness or similarity to be comfortable. We shy away from people who are different. Why?

Perhaps deep down we are insecure about ourselves. Or, perhaps opposites threaten us and excite a hostile or defensive attitude. Whatever the reason, we suffer when we allow differences to disturb or separate us from the varied religions and religious ideas. Our world is full of diversity. Differences constitute the strength of humanity and are a key to our survival. An old axiom puts it: "Better to be different in life than the same in death." Learn to respect and honor differences and you discover a key to a healthier and more satisfying life.

Christians at their best look forward to a fullness that we do not now possess. How can we in the name of Jesus Christ suppose that we are already in possession of fullness of truth? Jesus spoke of a kingdom of God that is not yet here in fullness. "It does not yet appear what we shall be . . ." We are on a journey, a spiritual journey, and have much to learn from others on that journey. We have not arrived and no one else has either. We need to help one another.

The Spirit of God moves in many ways and through many people and cultures. The Christian exclusivist denies himself/herself the full scope of revelation. How sad!

Something to think about.

A letter to the editor was critical about my newspaper series on uncertainty. Coming from a tradition that relies on "certainties," the writer's antipathy to uncertainty is understandable. To accept uncertainties throws one into a dependent status. Many, like Eve in the creation story, want certainty, want to be like God. The judgment of God comes to those who are tempted with certainty. The judgment takes the form of human traits that separate us from one another: rigidity, censoriousness, exclusiveness, and intransigence — to name a few.

But, yes, "You shall know the truth and the truth shall make you free." What is this truth? Not propositional truth! Not objective truth! Not dogmatic truth! This truth is not factual but relational. Such truth is revealed in a person. This truth we see in the life and ministry of Jesus. Is this certainty? Hardly! To follow Jesus in his life of loving response to those who were rejected by the religionists of his day, takes faith. The Christian life is not certainty; we do not live by sight but by faith. What society so desperately needs are models of compassionate love on the part of those who "know" themselves to be loved eternally. This knowledge is not factual but intuitive. This is a faith stance and not sight (certainty). The issue is the nature of truth. Factual truth is important for many aspects of life; but in Christianity (and some other religions), we do not have factual truth but, more significantly, relational truth. This truth saves us from the dogmatism that divides.

Something to think about.

QUESTIONS FOR THOUGHT AND DISCUSSION

1. How would you describe the kingdom of God?

2. What should be our relationship with other religions?

3. What did Jews take from other religions?

4. What did early Christian writers learn from others?

5. How do you feel about the different denominations in the Christian Church?

6. Do you embrace certainty in your religious convictions? Why or why not?

7. Why are we threatened by differences?

8. What do life's uncertainties mean to you?

CHAPTER 3

About Religion

I have heard it, and you have too: "A plague on all religions! They do more harm than good. Religion has fomented wars and divided societies. We can do without it."

Wait a minute. Everyone worships some god. Religion is ultimate concern. Whether it is work, pleasure, self, sex, family, security or some ideology, our religion is where we place our main focus. Whatever our religion, each one has its own ritualistic acts. Pay attention to sport events or family rituals and you will see what I mean.

Higher religions focus the individual away from narrow concern to something more lasting. The great religions produce symbols and stories by which to illuminate various aspects of life. But if such symbols and stories are reduced to static literalisms, they lose their purpose and become dull and prosaic. Religious fanaticism occurs when one makes absolute what is not. A leader becomes a god. A book or doctrine becomes the ultimate authority. The cults offer the best example of fanaticism. The ideology becomes absolute and not subject to doubt. A we/they polarity develops. A fortress mentality dominates the religion: we against the world. Such religion falsifies the rightful place of religion.

Something to think about.

On the last page, I raised the issue of religious fanaticism. Such religion leads to a loss of freedom. In the most extreme cases, people give up personal decision-making to the religious authority. This was dramatically evidenced in Jim Jones' Peoples' Temple and in David Koresh's Branch Davidians; but, we can also see it elsewhere. Dostoevsky was right: "Man is tormented by no greater anxiety than to find someone quickly to whom he can hand over that gift of freedom...."[1]

The cults help us to see the difference between a healthy and an unhealthy religion. A healthy religion retains a measure of its opposite—doubt. Authentic religious faith takes little to be absolute but probes everywhere and everything for "truth." An unhealthy religion has too much faith. Faith has gone wild. Adherents have either lost or never acquired critical doubt. Such religion is one with the cancer of certainty that in the end becomes selfdestructive.

All healthy religions have the responsibility to teach followers how to doubt; how to ask hard, critical questions; how to "test the fruits"; and how to keep open and in dialogue with those who think differently. A modicum of doubt is the life-saving companion to the mustard seed of faith or else fanaticism soon follows.

Something to think about.

---

1. *The Brothers Karamozov, Booke, Chapter 5*

When we look at cult movements, we see religious fanaticism. David Koresh was a deranged victim of his own messianic illusions. Fanaticism emerges the moment a religion minimizes or excludes all the ideas that confront or oppose it. The religious fanatic never sees issues and people as they are. Hatred and suspicion make such religionists fabricate demons. The fanatic hides from true debate; the concept of dialogue is alien. The fanatic has answers and not questions, certainties and not limited truths seeking for completion.

A healthy and beneficial religious expression requires the checks and balances of dialogue and interaction with those "outside." Some forms of Christian fundamentalism are like cults with a mind-set more than a body of beliefs. Such a mind-set is one of intolerance and inflexibility. We see this in some forms of orthodox Judaism as well as in Muslim and Christian fundamentalism.

The fundamentalist lens through which the fanatic sees the world is fear. But there is no need to fear. The love of God frees us from fear. There is no fear in love for perfect love cast out fear. The healthy Christian strategy is to eliminate enemies by loving them into friends, but how hard it is for us to do that. Yet, in this day of religious strife, we must try.

Something to think about.

What is constructive religion? That is the question with which we closed the last page. The answer seems complex but is really quite simple. Constructive religion is being absolutely related to the Absolute and relatively related to all the relativities of life. God, by whatever name, is the one absolute: all else (the Bible, doctrine, mate, children, parents, work, health, nation, etc.) is relative. When we absolutize a relative good, we are in trouble. This is what the Religious Right does with the Bible, doctrinal statements, and moral precepts. This is properly called idolatry. The consequent judgment takes the form of paranoia, suspicion, divisiveness, censoriousness, hostility and loss of dialogue and civility.

A constructive religion that absolutizes only the Absolute holds no absolute doctrines, concepts or ideas but allows critical thinking with nothing off limits. Such religion maintains the provisional nature of beliefs. Adherents give interim assent to religious beliefs that commend themselves and act on them. At the same time they keep open to the possibility that any doctrine or ethical value could be proved wrong, that in our pluralistic society we must respect the ideas and values of other religious positions and not be threatened by different views. This means that such a religion operates by faith and not sight, not certainty. Holding ones views as absolutely certain and beyond doubting leads to authoritarianism and finally repression.

Something to think about.

What is constructive religion that is not paranoid, divisive, hostile, censorious and lacking in civility? Such a religion holds to freedom of religion and even from religion for those who choose not to be formally religious. A constructive religion will champion the freedom of our country from political rule by religious forces. Religious influence, Yes; religious control, No! Religious control is what many of our forebears came to this country to avoid. A constructive religion comes to grips with economic, political, and moral issues by not simplifying the issues into neatly divided rights and wrongs, trusting in the process of free interaction, free discussion and free assembly.

The basic issue over against the Religious Right with its authoritarianism and absolutisms is: Can constructive religion transmit a living faith to successive generations? Can we see religion enabling us to deal with the ambiguities, tragedies, and crucial decisions that face us? Can we live trusting in a transcendent power that works in us, with us, between us, and at times in spite of us to bring justice and righteousness into our world? I am hopeful; but if the non-absolutists fail, the future may well rest with the Religious Right bringing a new repression. I shudder to think of what would happen to many of us if this movement succeeds in its agenda.

Something to think about.

Why has liberalism lost its appeal when its basic philosophy of fairness and justice has been so successful in formulating contemporary society? The problem, says James Wall, formerly with "The Christian Century," is that too many liberals have become fundamentalists in their orientation. Under the pressure of wanting answers, they have rejected ambiguities and denied the complexity of issues.

Too many today are unwilling to live with uncertainties and to struggle openly and respectfully with others to reach some accommodation on abortion, sexuality, civil rights, and gun control—to mention a few issues. Yet it is the liberal spirit that is most likely to contribute to a more just and humane society. Liberalism at its best is both optimistic and pragmatic. The liberal believes in improvement through change but not in perfectibility. Thus it is uniquely able to live in a state of progress toward that illusive goal.

Perhaps we should scrap the word "liberal" and focus on a new term: "Progressive Christianity." If Progressive Christianity (an outgrowth of liberalism) has anything to say, it grows out of a determination not to resort to overly simple or authoritarian answers. Yet it is just this that makes life exciting and dramatic. We live in a dynamic and ever-changing world, and we are not alone. Thanks be to God.

Something to think about.

What does it mean to be a person of faith in the midst of many faiths? This is a crucial question for our time. Religious animosity and outright hostility face us around the world. Religious minorities suffer persecution in many countries. Several religions make exclusivist claims for themselves which make dialogue with others next to impossible. Is this state inevitable, and do we just accept the fact of separate and antagonistic religions? What follows is the beginning of a series reflecting on the current state of religion.

As various religions confront each other, we discover the following reactions to the diversity:

No religion is true; all are equally deluded.
All religions are true but imperfectly so.
One religion is true and others are false.
One religion is true and others only partially true.
All religions are partially true.

The first position counts all religion as irrelevant and immaterial and not worth time and attention. The third position is the least dialogical and encourages animosity. The other positions offer some hope for dialogue and growth in understanding.

Something to think about.

We are continuing a word about religious tensions in our world. How do we understand our neighbors of different religions? Where do others fit in? For religious people, three responses come to mind:

1. Exclusivism — holding that one's tradition, doctrine, and belief are the only true ones;
2. Inclusivism — recognizing many communities of faith having apprehensions of truth and valid traditions but believing that one's own way is the culmination and takes in all the others;
3. Pluralism — seeing the value of diversity and contributing to the understanding that diversity need not be an obstacle but is part of God's providence in dealing with a diverse humanity.

What is happening today is the tension between a world-wide movement toward exclusivism alongside the necessity for interfaith dialogue if we are to have respect for one another and understand our differences. I'll leave it to your judgment as to what position is most in tune with God's will or, if you prefer, with harmony and good will on planet earth.

Something to think about.

The religious exclusivist is one of the main problems in the world today. Religious fundamentalism is found among Christians, Jews, Muslims, Buddhists and some others. Wherever it occurs we see extreme nationalism, authoritarianism, and absolutism. Dialogue with others is either non-existent or at a minimum. Why dialogue when you have the truth? Instead the effort is to control and manipulate. In the process, almost anything, can be justified. (For corroboration of all this read the multi-volume project of the National Academy of Arts and Sciences called the Fundamentalism Project. One volume, *Fundamentalisms Observed*, is in many local libraries.)

The inclusivists in religion do not see others as opposites. An open attitude prevails in which others are included. Yet, the conviction is that one's position is for everyone. For the Hindu, God has many names and faces and is not peculiar to the Hindu. Hindus believe that all would be better off to recognize this "truth." Christian inclusivists see their affirmations not just for Christians but for everyone. The new covenant supersedes all others. Muslim inclusivists see their position as superior to both that of Jews and Christians. The final revelation of God was to Mohammed. The Ba'hais include all in the final revelation and see this understanding as their gift.

The inclusivists are more benign than the exclusivists and are not defensive, militant, or especially triumphalist. Yet, they do not tend to listen to others nor learn from others. They do not as a rule challenge their own positions. What results is a measure of pride and self-satisfaction that raises barriers in human relationships. Is there not a better way?

Something to think about.

How can we understand religious diversity? Look with me at the pluralist position. The pluralist does not exclude nor include but interrelates and recognizes interdependence. The pluralists understand themselves in terms of diversity and take seriously other religions not as adversaries but as coreligionists living and relating together.

A revolution in theology is going on today which many of us see as the working of God in human community to bring harmony out of chaos. To those in tune with this movement, there is an awareness that in diversity we see more clearly the God around whom all re-ligions evolve. In this awareness we see and appreciate others on their own terms. The pluralist believes that it is not possible for one religion to have exclusive possession of all truth. Such a posi-tion encourages dialogue so needed in our time if we are to have peace on planet earth. In no way does the pluralist harbor disre-spect for his/her own tradition. Instead, the pluralist sees a partic-ular religion as a significant part of a much larger whole, which I shall elaborate on the next page.

Something to think about.

We have been considering religious diversity and have taken note of the problems presented by the exclusivist and inclusivist positions. On the other hand, the pluralist position encourages dialogue and interrelationship. What is pluralism in religion? Several things need to be said.

Pluralism is more than the fact of religious diversity. It is a nonadversarial way of seeing oneself in relation to other traditions. Pluralism is more than tolerating the existence of others; it wants to relate. And pluralism is more than a relativism that affirms that all are good with no ultimate value. Pluralism is also not syncretism, the attempt to mold together all religions into some bland common denominator. Pluralism is about the creation of relationships by recognizing what is valuable in other traditions and, at the same time, having the capacity to be critical of one's own religion. The tendency so often is to take the best of one's own faith and compare it with the worst in the faith of others.

Something to think about.

What is it we need to do in a society as religiously diverse as ours? A healthy religion can contribute to the health of society by:

1. Taking responsibility to know people of other traditions without the corruptions of ethnic or religious animosities;

2. Watching the tendency to stereotyping and bearing false witness;

3. Seeing differences not as threats but as learning possibilities:

   a. From Hindus, the use of all the senses in religious worship (touch, smell, sight, taste);
   b. From Muslims, multiple times of daily religious devotion in union with millions around the world;
   c. From Buddhists, the discipline of silence and practicing the clarity of presence;
   d. From Jews, sacred spaces built in time, shared with family and friends.

We need to expand the "We" so that we no longer do separately what we can do together (the works of justice and humanitarian ministries).

All this is pluralism as I see it. The wave of the future is already beating on our shore demanding something other than the animosities of the past, the exclusivism of the absolutists, and the isolationism of religions too narrowly defined. "Who has seen the wind (spirit)? Neither you nor I. But when leaves are trembling, the wind is passing by." (Christina Rossetti) I see movement of the leaves. How about you?

Something to think about.

What is the role of religion in relation to education? Higher education is leading us to the awareness that each person lives in organic union with all humanity and the entire spectrum of organic life. Religion's role is to add the transcendent dimension — the underlying purpose in having something and not nothing. Life on planet earth is more than an accidental collocation of atoms. We have a purposeful product of an evolutionary and developmental process that is creating a people with a universal consciousness. Such a people recognize a mutual interdependence between various peoples and nations. Behind the process is a "spirit" that cannot be relegated to simply physical processes.

Religion affirms the mystery of life and gives the mystery a name. Religion dares to affirm that the mystery was before us, is with us, and pushes us forward to a future of immense possibility. That mystery is lovingly for us which means that we can tolerate "the slings and arrows of outrageous fortune" because of a confidence that in everything there is a working for good. To the scholastic disciplines, religion contributes the element of basic trust in the kingdom that is both here and coming more fully. "Religious insights help to form the moral conviction that can guard against educating a race of clever apes."

Something to think about.

QUESTIONS FOR THOUGHT AND DISCUSSION

1. How would you define religion?

2. What is fanaticism in religion?

3. How would you define constructive religion?

4. How does the term "Progressive Christianity" cope with some aspects of traditional Christianity?

5. How do you understand the diversity in beliefs and customs of other religions?

6. How would you describe your religious orientation?

7. How can religion and education relate?

CHAPTER 4

About God

The Russian Christian Leo Tolstoy once said that God is life, everywhere in it and of it. Love of life is love of God who gives life. To despair of life and to dislike one's existence is an affront to God who is met in the midst of life. Dostoevsky, another Russian Christian, once exclaimed: "One must love life before loving its meaning; and when love of life disappears, no meaning can console us."

We face today myriads of people who do not love life. The violence in our society gives evidence that many are lashing out in despair at ever finding a fulfilling and meaningful existence. And when today's politics of meanness is intent on sacrificing the underprivileged for the sake of further benefits for the wealthy, I fear the increased level of despair. It is still true that the measure of any society is what happens to the least of those among us: the young, the sick, the poor, the elderly, and the minority.

Something to think about.

What flack has emerged in response to the Re-Imagining Conference held some time ago? The Presbyterians were torn asunder by the debate. Some Methodists were upset. Others, both pro and con, have gotten into the fray through letters to editors and magazine articles. So much ado about nothing! Why do I say that and what is the issue?

At the Conference the Greek word "sophia" was used in place of God. Why? Sophia means wisdom and is a synonym used for God in the Jewish Scriptures. Wisdom in Hebrew is a feminine term and feminists found this to be quite affirming. Those at the Conference were not worshipping some pagan god, nor were they being unbiblical. The Scriptures use many feminine images for God. God is neither male nor female but androgynous, having the qualities of both. The dominance of masculine language is an accident of history and not an absolute to bind all future generations.

How strange that we can call God "Rock of Ages" and in so doing refer to God as a mineral; but call God "Sophia" and anger emerges from all those who seem to think that the concept of God is threatened. After all, all language about God is analogical or symbolic. Words about God are not to be taken literally as if we have captured God in our conceptualizations. All our words simply point in the direction of the incomparable mystery of love. Since we have to talk about the Mystery, we do so using the best analogies, metaphors, and symbols available to us. Sophia (wisdom) is among the best. That the term is feminine is a blessing to feminists of which I, a male, am somewhat one.

Something to think about.

Tension exists in our society between the patriarchy that has dominated our culture in the past and the feminism that has emerged to challenge that patriarchy. We get set in certain stereotyping and become immovable in our attitudes and opinions. In a brief word, I want to add to the dialogue and, hopefully, not the confusion.

We are male and female, and there are differences. Women are more peaceful than men. Research has substantiated this in about every culture. Women are biologically more tied to nature than are men. From puberty on body softness, vulnerability, less muscular development, and the need to cooperate with nature mark the female. The male from puberty on experiences virility, strength, and muscular development leading him to contend more with nature and with others.

What does this mean? At least this: we need a blending of the two-the nurturing and caring qualities that emerge from the female closeness to nature and the contending, struggling aspects of male nature. This is not to say each does not have the characteristics of the other in some degree. The other is very much in each of us. But in business, international affairs, politics and other aspects of life, we are better off with both men and women participating. So this is a plea for the blending and equal inclusion of both in religion, politics, business, and international affairs. Thank God we are moving in that direction.

Something to think about.

Creation spirituality speaks about the God in everything and everything in God. If that is so, God is a reality that applies to more than religious language, exercises, and institutions. Some Christians are concerned that we are adapting to the standards of the world and losing our distinction as Christians. Some truth is here to be sure. When our culture, whatever its state, becomes the determinative factor in decision-making, we may have lost the transcendent reference that stands over-against culture.

On the other hand, if God (the transcendent) is present not only in religious activity but in secular life as well, then that secular life has the possibility of disclosing the activity of God. Religious people have a tendency to get myopic and see God only in the so-called religious sphere of life. With eyes open, God can be seen not only in the relationship between people and groups but in animal and vegetative life as well. We are saved from pantheism when we identify God with the Judeo-Christian story and realize that seeking love, reconciling love, forgiving love are elements in life not just religious life. What Christianity does is to give us a language by which to talk about what is.

Where is God? No where because God is nothing; God is no thing. Everything we can see, we can locate. God is no thing, but in all, with all and through all – closer to us than breathing and nearer than hands and feet. We can't locate God because to do so would be to try to use God like we use things. God is an elusive Presence that we know not by sight, sound, taste or smell but by faith.

Something to think about.

The French existentialist Albert Camus wrote: "If God didn't exist we would have to invent a divinity to save us from turning human being into idols." Idolatry is the main problem with humanity. We are time and again making absolute that which isn't. In the search for happiness and security we hold on possessively to a person, job, pleasure, hobby, or institution and try to make it the meaning-giver of our lives. If not that, we try to find our security in making the Bible, doctrine, or ethical precepts absolute. Idolatry, in whatever form, always brings suffering of one kind or another. The loss of any of the first group of "idols" brings intense grief, discouragement, or despair. The loss of any of the latter leads to self-righteousness, pride (that precedes a fall), divisiveness, and "judgmentalism."

How do we avoid such idolatry? Be absolutely related to the one absolute (God, by whatever name) and relatively related to all else. Most of the relativities of life are good but not God. Leave room for losing what you have, for discovering that your "certainties" are not so certain and leave room for others who may differ from you in ideas and opinions. You may, then, be open to some exciting surprises that God has in store for you.

Something to think about.

Martin Buber, Jewish scholar, somewhere wrote that theology is the menu and religion is the dinner. To say this another way, theology is talking about God and religion is experiencing God. This is worth some thought.

Religious people do too much talking about God. We move into our heads and speak about who God is and what God does or does not do. We are more reluctant to share experiences of God. Yet, here is where we might find a common life.

Religion is awe before the mystery of life. Here and there, now and then, we are awe-struck: in a personal relationship, a nature experience, a piece of music, or a passage of literature. Religion is a sense of unworthiness before one of life's gifts: a new birth, a physical healing, the love of another. Religion is gratitude following being forgiven, accepted, or valued. Religion is that reaching out toward what is not "I" nor any other part of creation. Religion is life's experiences with the pneuma or God.

Something to think about.

QUESTIONS FOR THOUGHT AND DISCUSSION

1. How would you define God?

2. What is the relationship between violence and love of life?

3. What do you feel about feminine images for God?

4. How do you respond to the difference between female and male development?

5. How is the concept of God related to other than the religious sphere?

6. Idolatry is present today and maybe in you. What do we tend to make idols?

7. How is religion related to life experiences?

CHAPTER 5

About Jews and The Jesus Story

A Southern Baptist resolution (sometime ago) making evangelizing the Jews a high priority is most tragic. At least that is how such an action appears to me and many others. The resolution fails to recognize the integrity of the Jewish faith. We were taken back by unfortunate and hasty word of a Baptist pastor that God does not hear the prayer of a Jew. Think what that means! The prayers of the Psalmist, those of Jesus, and the prayers of thousands of rabbis and faithful Jewish people have been of no account. Such presumption and such arrogance!

What do such words do to Jewish-Christian relationships? If taken seriously, such a stance would take us back a few hundred years. A new wind is stirring. A new attitude is bringing many of us to a more open and understanding perspective. What Jesus has done for Gentiles is to open the concept of the People of God to include us. We have been brought into a faith that includes Abraham and Sarah, Isaac and Rebecca, Jacob and Rachel, and all the prophets.

The uniqueness of Jesus is that he broke down the wall separating Jew and Gentile. We are the People of God, and the name of Jesus unites us. The name Jesus means God saves or God will save. That is the monistic faith uniting us. To use the name of Jesus or the person of Jesus to separate us is indeed presumption and arrogance. And I know all the Scripture verses that literalists can use to counter this. I simply plead for us to look at the life and ministry of Jesus and ask whether the resolution above is in harmony with what we see.

Something to think about.

What do we Gentiles think about Jews? We are constantly amazed at the number of the great scientists, mathematicians, philosophers, theologians, and musicians who are Jews. The outside world does not know quite what to do with this fact. Perhaps the gifts that Jews bring to society are related to a sensitivity that comes from years of persecution and oppression. No people have experienced the measure of physical and psychological pain as have the Jews. No people are more familiar with the inhumanity rampant in the world.

At the same time, no group of people has been more intent and obsessed with finding answers to injustice. Perhaps this is one way to understand Steven Spielberg's film, *Schindler's List*, one of the most powerful presentations in many a decade. If any Gentile wants to enter into Jewish life to gain some understanding of what has happened to Jews, get the film.

What all this may mean is that the One who works to make some good emerge from all things has taken what the world has done and brought some compensation to the lives of Jews. In no way does this justify what has happened in the past, but it has raised a people who manage, in spite of all, to produce people to be a blessing to others. What is this but the promise to Abraham: "I will bless you and make you a blessing to the whole world."

Something to think about.

In the Jesus story, he appears as the most perfect expression of the moral and religious quest. He is also the most complete and perfect expression of God. Christian theology has always held to the full humanity as well as the divinity of Jesus. Both expressions are at the heart of Christianity. As fully human, Jesus as a Jew is the representative of the best of humanity; and the Christian affirmation is that he is the best expression of the nature of God. Both are proclamations not facts.

Likewise, Jesus is not the answer to our questions, but the questioner. "Who do you say that I am?" Do you love me?" "Who is your neighbor?" Many more questions may come to mind. Jesus prompts us to respond to such questions with our lives. For Jesus to be the answer, we raise the questions. I think that the opposite is more true.

Many go to the Bible to find absolute truth. But this misses the fact that words are not themselves absolute. They are arrows shot at a distant target that inevitably fall short of the mark. This is especially true of the biblical words that point to the mystery we call God. To imbue words with absolute authority is bibliolatry (a word that literalists and absolutists do not like). The Holy Spirit, God's Spirit, is still the authority to which the Scriptures bear witness. But God is not dead so that we are confined to one or even 66 expressions of the mind and heart of God. The Bible is our primary text but not the repository of absolute truths which cannot be expressed with words alone. The truth about love is not found in any words but in persons and ultimately in God.

Something to think about.

For Christianity, Lent is the time to prepare for Easter focusing on aspects of the life of Jesus. Strange how this life lived so long ago offers so many insights into right ways of living today!

How did Jesus gain his friends, for instance? He did not begin by telling them how much he knew. Basically he did not try to argue people into a relationship. He did not push but attracted people by the depth of his concern for them. Jesus was in touch with a principle of motivation: people want to know how much you care before they care how much you know.

One account suggests that Jesus on Wednesday of Holy Week went to the home of Mary and Martha in Bethany. He had a need for friends and a place to relax. Friends are people with whom we feel at home. So with Jesus and so with us.

Many try to live their lives as though they have no need for others. We tend to praise independence as if that were higher than dependence. Not so! The best life is a blending of the two: independence enough to make decisions and take action and dependence enough to know support and affirmation. We all have needs. To express those needs and to allow others to help meet those needs is the substance of community building.

Jesus had needs. On that Wednesday he went to Bethany and spent a quiet day with friends. He reached out for understanding and support. I believe he found it.

Something to think about.

Easter, as a part of the Jesus story, has a strange drawing power. Yes, tradition and habit play parts in Easter church attendance. At the same time, I think something more is going on. We are so aware of the transience of life. All that we see is destined for destruction and decay. Easter somehow puts us in touch with eternity.

The word resurrection, in spite of the bodily and fleshly connotations of the word, speaks to our deepest hopes and aspirations. We need to be reminded that death is not the last word but life is. We tend to get discouraged at times by what we see in our personal and national life. Truth at times seems to be on the scaffold and wrong appears on the throne; but the Easter message beckons us to a deeper look. Whatever we may believe about Jesus' resurrection (and Christians vary greatly about what they give intellectual assent to), we gather on Easter to be reminded that " . . . we look not to the things that are seen but to the things that are unseen; for the things that are seen are transient, but the things that are unseen are eternal."(2 Cor. 4:18) Easter says not death, not an ending, not defeat but victory and a new beginning. So it is about life seen through the eyes of faith.

Something to think about.

In the Jesus Christ story we find a positive force working for good. How many lives have been changed and how much good has been done because of the influence of this one historical Jewish figure! What is going on here?

Think of light and darkness. Light is positive and darkness is negative. Darkness is the absence of light. Light works to overcome darkness. Good and evil have a similar relationship. Good is positive and evil, of course, is negative. Good is working to contribute to life; and evil works to destroy life. Just as darkness is no thing and would have no reality apart from light, so evil only exists in opposition to good. God is the supreme good working for us and Satan is the personification of the nothing that is in opposition to God. Satan has no reality apart from God.

Since Jesus offers newness of life, empowers life, changes life, ennobles life and constantly directs us to fullness of life, Jesus is of God bringing us from darkness to light—such is the Christian affirmation.

Something to think about.

What has happened through the centuries to Christianity? Here and there it would seem that the Jewish religion of Jesus has been replaced by a religion about Jesus. To be sure that we do not replace one with the other, we need to see them separately.

The religion of Jesus is quite clear from the Synoptic Gospels (Matthew, Mark, and Luke). His religion is nothing less than the love of God and love of neighbor tied together. This is Judaism at its best. He holds to no privatized religion, a my God and I perspective. No relationship to God can be right apart from the right relationship to the neighbor. This is where we all fall short. When our relation to others is faulty, our relationship to God suffers accordingly. Our faith journey involves the two together. We are not left with much room for self-satisfaction. In fact, most of us live by forgiveness for our relational failures which gives us the courage and determination to keep on the journey.

The religion about Jesus focuses on a transaction whereby Jesus saves us by his suffering and death. As sometimes presented, this is divorced from one's relationship to others and is a purely personal matter. In the religion about Jesus, Jesus is the Messiah, the Logos, the pre-existent Son (all metaphors borrowed from other cultures) who intervened in human life to do for us what we could not do for ourselves. How easy it is to separate this from the Jewish religion of Jesus. Jesus plays a definitive role in our lives by offering us a religion (or more correctly, a way of life) that involves love of God (life) and love of neighbor.

Something to think about.

New insights have emerged lately about the religion of Jesus. We know that Christians during the first three centuries were called "People of the Way." That "Way" was following Jesus's life style of compassion and non violence. However, sometime between 70 C.E. and 85 C.E. birth stories about Jesus were formed by the Christian community. This was the beginning of a religion about Jesus that became fully formed by 367 C.E. with the Council of Nicea. As one author has put it: "The Nicene Creed replaced the Sermon on the Mount."

For centuries the religion about Jesus seemed to take priority over the religion of Jesus. Here and there some Christians tried to impose the religion of Jesus over doctrines about Jesus but to no avail. Thomas Jefferson, a product of the 17th – 18th centuries move-ment called the Enlightenment, took the Christian Scriptures and cut out the virgin birth, miracles, and resurrection and called it "The Philosophy of Jesus of Nazareth." His reason could not abide the deification of Jesus. He became the forerunner of the recovery of the religion of Jesus. Jefferson's efforts were strangely predated by a document called the Gospel of Thomas. What a surprise ac-companied this discovery giving us-

Something to think about.

When Bishop Athanasius and Emperor Constantine got together to unify the Christian movement, multiple volumes of gospels and other Christian writings were in existence. One such document was the Gospel of Thomas. In the mid 3rd century Hipolytus, aware of this gospel designated it as heresy. When Athanasius posted the 27 books he accepted as authoritative, the Gospel of Thomas was not part of the list. He ordered Thomas all other literature to be destroyed. Some monks in Egypt disagreed with the bishop and placing the documents in clay jars buried them in the sands of Egypt where they were not found until 1945.

Years later these documents were finally made available to scholars. The Gospel of Thomas has proved to be the most significant of the findings. Scholars think it was written between 50 and 62 C.E. (formerly A.D.). They believe that Thomas, some 20 years following the death of Jesus, brought together a number of people who had heard Jesus, and he wrote down what they remembered. The result was 114 sayings with no virgin birth, no miracles, and no resurrection. It seems that all of the latter were added to Christian literature later.

Think what this means. The earliest writings present Jesus as a Jewish sage, teacher, and prophet of social righteousness in whom many found God represented. The earliest known Gospel presented the religion of Jesus and not the religion about Jesus.

Something to think about.

QUESTIONS FOR THOUGHT AND DISCUSSION

1. What is the Christian relationship to Judaism?

2. What Jews have made contributions to your life?

3. Can you accept the understanding that terms used to describe Jesus are proclamations and not facts? What does that mean to you?

4. How does the term Progressive Christianity cope with some aspects of traditional Christianity?

5. How do you understand the diversity in beliefs and customs of others religions?

6. How would you describe your religious orientation?

7. How can religion and education relate?

CHAPTER 6

About Mythology

Why is the word "mythology" so troublesome to some people? Mythology is an appropriate word for certain kinds of literature. The word does not mean false or untrue. Neither does it necessarily mean truth. The latter all depends. Truth has at least two forms: (1) factual, provable truth or, (2) personal, existential truth. Mythology often deals with the latter.

Mythology began as pre-historical writing. How did people understand the beginnings of things before there were any records? No discipline called science was available with the research possibilities of digging into the past. Primitive memory, intuitive assumptions, and, yes, even spiritual revelation played a role. Answers came as creative people used their own inner resources. Some wrote aesthetic myths whose purpose was entertainment. Others wrote explanatory myths to answer natural questions. How strange to study ancient myths from various cultures and see similarities! The coming into being of humanity is an example. Greek and Roman mythology speaks of the Titan, Prometheus, who molded a figure out of clay in the image of the gods and breathed life into it. In the Babylonian Epic of Creation humanity is cursed by the gods for corrupting the purity of creation. Again in Roman/Greek mythology Jupiter deals with evil in the world with a great rain resulting in a flood that covered the earth. Only virtuous Deucalion and Pyrra were left to repeople the earth. The comparison with Genesis is striking. Are these all myths while Genesis is facts? Or do these sections of Genesis share in the common genre called mythology, dealing with truth at a deeper level than facticity?

Something to think about.

The last page introduced the subject of mythology, a type of literature with its origin in the ancient world. Many cultures raised questions about beginnings and had similar answers. Stories from Greeks and Romans, Babylonians and Hebrews share great similarities. Other cultures could be mentioned as well. In all these stories we are dealing with more than facts (the biblical stories as well). The truth in these stories moves at a deeper level.

With the coming of history, mythology did not end. When human beings want to move past fact to a deeper meaning, they use the language of mythology (story form), poetry (symbolic writing), fable (animals speaking), or drama (stage setting with characters and conversation). Is the Bible myth? No! Does the Bible contain myths? Yes, the second story of creation, for example! Is the Bible poetry? No! Does the Bible contain poetry? Yes, Psalms, for instance. Is the Bible fable? Of course not! Does the Bible have fables? Yes, the talking snake in Genesis 3 and Balaam's ass, Numbers 22! Is the Bible drama? No! Does the Bible contain drama? Yes, Job! Is the Bible allegory? No! Does the Bible contain allegories? Yes, Jonah and others!

The obsession with facticity prevents many from seeing the richness of the Bible that is much more concerned with personal, existential truth than with facts.

Something to think about.

Why does "myth" have to be a red-flag word for some? I plead: Do not let it be. Myth, fable, poetry, drama, and allegory are all related. They do not deal with fact but with the deeper level of personal meaning.

In Genesis 2, did God literally take up dirt (clay) and form it into a human being and breath into the molded, form the breath of life—literally? I have to say, of course not! Are we products of God's creative power? Yes! Do we have affinities with the earth and water, the natural elements? Of course! Did a snake literally talk to Eve? In what language? Or, is this a fable getting at the human temptation to be God? The story is true without having to be factual.

Some say that Jesus believed in a literal creation story, Adam and Eve, Jonah, and Job. How do they know that? The first century was within a highly mythological age. Many mythological people were talked about as though they were real. Dionysus was torn apart and resurrected by Zeus to be divine. Osiris was a human being and like Dionysus was torn apart and then made divine by Isis. The world has been filled with story tellers who communicate valid insights into human life in other than factual terms.

How many talk about Hamlet or King Lear as though their stories were factual? Or, Dante's historical characters who were made into mythological figures confined to various levels of hell? Be grateful for truths about life that come from many sources. But insist that all in the Bible is factual and you miss the profundity in the literature. Energy is expended in defending facticity and the personal truth is lost in the process.

Something to think about.

We have been looking at mythology as a good word referring to writing that is not dealing with history and facts but with meanings. The Bible, as with all ancient literature, made use of mythology as well as other forms of literature.

How about the New Testament? Are the miracle stories all facts, historical events? I don't think so; but I must confess that I cannot be sure about this. Am I just supposed to believe all these stories as facts no matter what? Why? The meaning of these stories is not based on their facticity. The Gospel writers told the Jesus story in relation to the exodus story (paradigm). Jesus went down into the water and came up out of the water (like the Hebrews and the Red Sea). Jesus went into the wilderness for 40 days (like the wilderness wanderings of the Hebrews). Jesus fed the 5,000 (like the Hebrews were fed in the wilderness). And there are other parallels. The author was saying in symbolic fashion that Jesus was another of God's Exodus events freeing people from slavery.

The story is told in John (John 5:1-8) of a man who had been ill for 38 years and was waiting to get into a pool and experience the water's supposed healing properties. Jesus asked him if he wanted to be healed. The man proceeded to complain that no one was helping him to get down to the pool and others were getting there first. He was a malcontent. Jesus told him to pick up his pallet and walk. He was healed. Fact? I doubt it. True? Yes, I have experienced that word from Jesus. This story was not told to prove that Jesus was the Son of God or that this is the way to be healed of ailments. The truth is that the Lord of Life is telling us to pick up our life situation, the agendas that life has given us, and live with them. We can be healed: true then, and true now. Fact? I don't know; but the facticity is irrelevant to the real truth.

Something to think about.

QUESTIONS FOR THOUGHT AND DISCUSSION

1. What does mythology mean to you?

2. Do you know myths that are true meaningfully but not factually?

3. What various literary forms are in the Bible?

4. What is the difference between factual truth and existential truth?

CHAPTER 7

About Liberty and Freedom

July is the month in which we celebrate our freedoms. But what is freedom? A recent biography of the eminent jurist, Learned Hand, has a quote that I want to reflect on piecemeal on several pages. Here is the first.

"The spirit of liberty is the spirit that is not too sure that it is right; . . ." What does it mean to be certain? The aura of certainty tends to lead one not to be open to listening to others. Why listen to others when you "know" you have the truth? Why enter into real dialogue when you are right and the other is wrong? Dialogue involves a give and take; but if you have all the truth, you have nothing to gain from others. Certainty breeds self-righteousness and pride. In your next argument or intense discussion when you begin to harbor some doubt about whether or not you are right, don't be embarrassed but grateful. You may be listening and open to some growing. This is the spirit of liberty.

Something to think about.

To continue a quote from Judge Learned Hand: " . . . the spirit of liberty is the spirit which seeks to understand the minds of other men and women; . . ." When one is certain, the impetus to understand the position of another is severely weakened. Certainty breeds separation, and separation is sin—to use a classic definition of the word. When one entertains the possibility of being wrong, an openness develops toward the ideas of others. This leads to the possibility of growth.

How true this is in relation to other religions. To hold that one's religion has the whole truth and nothing but the truth closes the door to understanding the thoughts and ways of others. Much of the hostility and animosity in the world rests right here. The problem with religious fanaticism or fundamentalism is the closed mind toward other religions. This is a tragic separation.

Something to think about.

Judge Learned Hand again: "..., the spirit of liberty is the spirit that weighs their (others') interests alongside its own without bias; ..." What is it we see in the Jesus of history? Openness to others — especially those rejected or demeaned by the religious people of his day (lepers, foreigners, tax collectors, women, etc.) Some forms of Christianity appear not to give attention to the interests of others but are obsessive about their own narrow agenda (anti-choice in abortion, anti homosexual rights, anti feminism, anti pluralism, etc,) Hear a word from the Gospel of John: "So if the Son makes you free, you will be free indeed." The Son, Jesus, makes us free from sin (separation from others) by both example and empowering us to go and do likewise.

We call Jesus Savior not because of some abstract transaction in the heavenly regions but because his life gives us a pattern of what being fully human is all about. More can be said about this but not less.

Something to think about.

One last reflection on the words of Judge Learned Hand: ". . . the spirit of liberty is the spirit of Him who, near two thousand years ago, taught mankind (sic) that lesson it has never learned, but has never quite forgotten, that there may be a kingdom where the least shall be heard and considered side by side with the greatest."

Minus that spirit, we are intent on maintaining the status quo that blesses us while others are deprived by the injustices of many of our systems. Is this not behind the objections to universal coverage in health care when almost forty million people are not covered? Many are intent on keeping our affluent lifestyle at the expense of the lives and well-being of others. We too often protest the taxes that try to equalize the living field. Meanwhile the millionaires and billionaires double and quadruple while the poor get poorer. History tells us what happens when such a state continues.

Something to think about.

QUESTIONS FOR THOUGHT AND DISCUSSION

1. What does liberty mean to you?

2. What is the problem in living religiously with certainty?

3. To what extent are we satisfied with the way things are when so many are deprived of health and well being?

About Ethics

How do we make ethical decisions? By law or by love? That's the issue between those who hold to ethical absolutes and others who are more situationally oriented. Consider the reasoning of one who is attracted more to situation ethics than to absolute ethic.

Does God sit somewhere on high giving absolute moral laws with no concern about specific human situations? Not so! God is not "up there" but "in here," within, between, and among us. God is in community. The pressure toward reconciliation, forgiveness, mercy, and compassion comes from the activity of the one absolute, God. The issue for ethics is: What is the loving thing to do in a specific situation? That is not always an easy question to answer. Life often contends with life, and what may be loving to one may be unloving to another. Placing an elderly invalid, perhaps an Alzheimer afflicted person, in a nursing home may appear to be unloving to the aged person but may be the loving thing to do in relation to a number of others in the family.

The abortion issue is similar. The decision to abort may be unloving when the issue is inconvenience or gender selection but be very loving when considering a thirteen year old girl or a conception by rape or incest. We may say that this is very unloving to an embryo or even a fetus (Neither is a baby!); but compared to loving a rational, fully formed human, this should be a non issue. The larger community is closer to the truth than the ethical absolutists who would outlaw abortion. The dominant opinion, I believe, is more in harmony with a God who is involved in human life, who is not some abstract and removed being pontificating ethical absolutes.

Something to think about.

If ethical decisions are best looked at situationally (as mentioned on the last page), what is the role of rules or laws?

The poet James Russell Lowell put it, "New occasions teach new duties, Time makes ancient good uncouth; .... " A bit of poetic license here because this could be true at times but hardly always. We do have much benefit from those who have preceded us. We are not cut flowers without roots. We have come out of the past and bring the past with us into the present. The past is present not to dominate us, not to govern us, not to enslave us, but to inform and enlighten us. Think about what this means.

The past's rules and laws can be of great help to us. We do not have to approach each situation "de novo." Our religious, political, and cultural heritages are available whenever we need them. They are like railings on stairs. We can at times proceed without them; but if we stumble, how good it is to reach out and find something there to give us stability. Laws and rules are like that. But to absolutize them is to be so bound to the past that we are likely to replace love with law and miss doing the loving thing. Responsible ethical decisions involve more than asking what the book says be it the Bible or law books.

Something to think about.

Once we knew, or thought we did. Right and wrong seemed so clear. The old morality (what constituted doing good) was circumscribed by commandments and teachings forming a prescribed set of do's and don'ts. Church people, for the most part, lived with a set of moral absolutes which they believed came from God. The commandments formed the roots, and the teachings of Jesus constituted the branches of our moral tree. Certain things were always wrong and we knew it. Now we are not so sure.

In Roman Catholic moral theology, marriage was indissoluble, not "ought not" but "cannot" be dissolved. Protestant sensitivities were not too far behind. But this meant that divorce was always wrong. How many today believe the "cannot" or even the "ought not"? Moving from the negative to the positive, honesty and truthfulness were always right. But military people made captive by an adversary were quizzed for information. Should they tell the truth? Or, following exploratory surgery, patients, discovered to be terminally ill, want to know the prognosis. Should they be told the truth right away or when they are stronger? Honesty is not always the best policy.

What has happened to us? Have we moved toward greater health or into a disruptive sickness?

Something to think about.

We are examining ethics in a world where decisions are not as clear-cut as they used to be. "You shall do no murder," the commandment says. But Dietrich Bonhoeffer, the noted German theologian-pastor, participated in the plot to kill Hitler. He was well versed in Judeo-Christian ethics. Somehow his decision seemed right even though the plot failed.

The legalism of the Pharisee, a book ethic supranaturally disclosed, seems more and more fractured in contemporary life. The heteronomous moral standards derived from God hardly seem adequate to cope with life's complexities. But we are troubled. The absolutes give us security. Decision-making is minimized. Doing right is going by the book. Isn't it?

The awful truth has struck home for many people. The absolutes are not self-authenticating. We are questioning the old so-called absolutes one after another. We have been enslaved to externally imposed moral standards counter to our experiences. The book gives us no word about why something is wrong; and those who legalistically follow ethical standards imposed from outside, appear too often as self-righteous prudes. Legalists are often cautious and defensive without trusting in their own goodness or the goodness of others.

No wonder a new morality came into being that rebelled from legalism into a self-directed mode. But, we shall see later, this has not been the solution to ethics either.

Something to think about.

The old morality of rules and laws has been replaced here and there by a new morality where everything has become relative and situational. The revolt against legalism has given us an autonomous ethic emerging from whatever the self wants or needs. This has led us to look into the inner self to discover the values that lie inside us. In the process a new danger has emerged — libertinism. Each one doing his or her own thing has produced an ethic of self-indulgence, arbitrariness, and immediacy (emerging from the mood of the moment). What we are seeing here and there is an infantile contempt for the law and few restraints. Self-discipline appears as needlessly restrictive of the good life.

What we have with the new morality is a new slavery — slavery to a self-will dominated by hedonism. T. S. Eliot has captured such an ethic in these words from "Choruses from the Rock,":

"And no one knows or cares who is his neighbor
Unless his neighbor makes too much disturbance,
But all dash to and fro in motor cars,
Familiar with the roads and settled nowhere."

Is the choice between the old morality of laws and commandments or the new morality of self-indulgence? Hardly! We are in a struggle to find a healthy alternative. I think the Church is uniquely equipped to provide that alternative when we turn to an incarnational theology and are sensitive to the presence of a Spirit known only in community. To that we shall turn on the next page.

Something to think about.

Where can we find an ethic to meet the needs of our day? Not in the legalisms of the past nor in the self-indulgence of present life. The alternative is an ethic that flows out of our life in community. Such an ethic is a product of relationships, what happens between us as individuals and groups.

This ethic is based on the presence of God, or better, the incarnation. What we call God has entered human life and is discovered not just within us but between us. God pressures us through events. God deals with us through others, comes to us in others, and is disclosed in the dynamics of relationships. I have no isolated relationship with another. If I think so, I will be tempted to use another for my own ends. Between us is always the activity of God that Christians call Christ, but other religions refer to this reality in other ways. This is more than my needs and desires. The question is: What is God intending in this relationship?

Within this context I am free to decide and this is scary. No wonder we are tempted to escape into legalism or into our own immediate wants. Freedom is at times a heavy burden, but it is the glory of humanity. When we choose in relationship to what is becoming, what God is bringing to pass, we are in harmony with our true self — a self in relationship to God through others.

Something to think about.

Ethics does not have to mean laws and commandments. And ethics is not rightfully one's own personal desires. What is going on between us? What is that kingdom which is working to become reality in human life? We are examining an ethic that is more than legalism and not simply self-determined. Yet, the moral codes, laws, and teachings have a place. They are dykes of love in a loveless world, as J.A.T. Robinson wrote. Laws are needed for children and we are all, time and again, children.

As mentioned previously, laws are like railings on the stairway, to be used as needed. We don't have to make every decision anew. More than that we can give attention to our own needs and wants but only as part of a larger picture. An ethic of community stands ready to break out of pre-established moral structures or self-determined needs and respond to a Spirit between us.

What such an ethic means is not yet fully developed but it has more possibilities for health and wholeness than legalism or self-indulgence. In this day when we are discovering the loss of old absolutes and the emptiness of autonomy, can we be open to the Spirit? The future that can be holds the exciting possibility of human freedom exercised within communities of mutually responsible people. What is this but the activity of God, the emergence of the kingdom in our midst.

Something to think about.

We can, therefore, we should. This has been the thinking of many about producing atomic weapons, altering genes, cloning, or making use of other scientific possibilities. But our modern world is crying for us to think ahead to the implications in the long run for actions taken today.

We can, but should we? What are our values? What are our priorities? What should we do based on some criteria other than we can? The time is now to reject any productions that threaten the life process or tend to dehumanize persons. And it is past time for us to consider what our actions are doing to the environment. What we need is an intuition generated by a great love for humanity as well as a loving care for the resources of planet earth. The fact that we can is no longer sufficient reason for doing anything. Humans are able to take a long look and imagine the implications of actions. At times we need to say that we can but we won't.

Something to think about.

QUESTIONS FOR THOUGHT AND DISCUSSION

1. What is the difference between absolute and situational ethics?

2. What do rules and laws do for us?

3. Are there many acts that are always wrong?

4. When have you questioned so-called absolute ethical laws?

5. What is the problem with self-directed ethics?

6. How can God be related to our ethical discussions?

7. If we can, scientifically or personally, should we?

About Government

Something is drastically wrong with us. This seems to be the growing conviction of many. Congressional members are retiring because they sense that something is wrong in our government. Private citizens are buying guns in record numbers. Security companies are experiencing a boom in their business. Prisons are overcrowded; crime is rampant; unemployment works havoc in families and communities.

No one has the complete answer; our situation is complex. Yet, we have some pointers in the direction of the problem and the solution. For some time now we have been programmed for egocentricity and self-survival. We have turned a blind eye to collective survival. We have lived believing that our physical, mental, and emotional needs could be met with financial security. We have been conditioned to think that each one is on his own and the object is to get, get, get. So the people with power are getting more and more, and those without are receiving less and less. There has been little "trickle down." The flow is up as the million and billionaires multiply. It is time to awaken to Jesus' admonition that the greatest of all is the servant of all. Not my needs but needs! Not my survival but ours!

Something to think about.

The budget crisis has everyone a bit confused. How can such an impasse happen? Two diametrically opposed philosophies are in conflict. The issues are complex. While what follows is an oversimplification, what I have to say warrants some thought — I think.

One pole is primarily dominated by economic criteria. The other is focused more on humanitarian concerns. Neither side is oblivious to the merits of the other's focus; but when "the chips are down," each pole reverts to its primary concern.

We appear to be living at a time when economic determinism is dominating humanitarian concerns. This does not bode well for the future. No society can long be sustained that neglects the weakest and poorest within its borders. Reasonable justice means that we cannot have extremely poor people and extremely rich people with a deteriorating middle. When this is so, a society becomes heartless and violence becomes a way of life. The present budget impasse may well be a struggle for the soul of our country.

Something to think about.

Why do people do what they do? Through the years we have seen sit-ins, marches, demonstrations, and vigils. Did they do any good? I am writing on Martin Luther King's birthday and in recognition that changes have come in our society and some of them by civil disobedience (from the Boston Tea Party through Rosa Parks to nuclear weapons and power protests). Results are always good to see, but benefits accrue whether we see outward changes or not.

Years ago a reporter asked A. J. Muste, a Quaker peace activist, if he thought that his all night vigil with a candle outside the White House was going to change the country's policies on Vietnam. He replied: "Oh, I don't do this to change the country. I do this so the country won't change me."

In our day of economic determinism and a politics of meanness, we need to find ways to protest so that we shall not be corrupted in the process. Unfortunately, it is easier to go along than to counter the bitterness and censoriousness of politics today.

Something to think about.

Election days come and go. Some of us may be pleased with an outcome. Others are likely disappointed. This is the way with elections. Some, however, seem especially divisive. The pre-election ads and speeches are disturbing. So much negativity and censoriousness! We see very little grace toward opponents. What are we to make of all this?

We could well remember the psalmist's word: "Put not your trust in princes, in a son of man in whom there is no help." (Ps. 146:3) This can be transvaluated by saying "Put not your trust in elected officials." The best of us can be caught up in systemic evil, saying and doing things as part of a system that we would not do alone. The mystery of it all is that our political process seems to work in spite of the system. Our two parties create a check and balance. The difficulty in getting something done is balanced by the restraint of not acting precipitously.

Trust, or should we say faith, is not in our systems but in that Reality that holds us together, works between us, and at times in spite of us to bring good to pass. Or, in the words of the psalmist again: "It is better to take refuge in the Lord than to put our confidence in princes." (Ps. 118:9) However we are reacting to elections, I think most of us can say that it isn't all bad.

Something to think about.

Conservatism won a resounding victory in the election of 2010. Everyone says that the victory reflects the mood of the country. This could well be, although many factors are involved in the election results. Many will take credit for the victory. The Religious Right certainly had a part in the conservative take-over, although many Republicans are not in sympathy with a large part of the Right's agenda. The climate in our nation seems amenable to a new authoritarianism and the Religious Right is laying a presumptuous claim to the chair and gavel.

Those who do not share the Christian Right's agenda or special brand of Christianity are left with a dilemma. Do we engage in confrontation or make an attempt at cooperation with those boards and offices oriented to Religious Right? I think something more is called for than a fight. All antagonists simply confirm their oppositionalism. We can begin with empathy and sensitivity to some of their concerns. Many of their concerns are legitimate: family life, the moral breakdown of society, crime, drug and alcohol abuse and the like. We can recognize that their authoritarianism represents a sickness that needs to be healed. Their absolutisms place a cancer of intolerance in our society. In the 19th century John Stuart Mill "bemoaned the propensity of religious people toward intolerance." The Religious Right with its absolutes is especially guilty. The key to healing and health is found in Alexis de Tocqueville's *Democracy in America* where he stated: "The influence of tyrannical religion must be countered by the resources of constructive religion." What is constructive religion? That will be our next subject.

Something to think about.

We seem to be in a negative mood about the federal government. Trashing government is in vogue. It would seem that government does nothing right. Perhaps we need to pause a moment and think about what we are doing.

How can we say that government is bad as we drive on the interstate highways of our nation? How can we say that our government is derelict when we have parents and other relatives past middle age that regularly and efficiently are paid the social security they deserve? How can we trash government when we fly in planes directed by flight controllers paid by the government who do an amazing job when we consider the extent of the traffic? Would we be better off without civil rights laws and nothing but state militias to guarantee our defense?

Governing is still a good word and the current administration has an admirable record of success in spite of all the trashing. The trashing not only adversely affects our nation, it places individuals in a negative spiral of discontent from which they may never emerge. How tragic!

Something to think about.

Congressional sessions are newsworthy. Where are they going? What legislation emerges? What will be happening to us as a people? To be more pointed: Where is the passion?

At first glance the passion in the congress seems to be rather narrowly defined as a capital gains tax cut, increased defense spending, prayer in the public schools, and welfare cuts among other things. As a Christian, I look to Jesus for an example of passionate concern. In the Parable of the Last Judgment (Matt. 25:31 ft), we see a reflection of his passion. Jesus identifies with the least among us and asserts that right living involves these identifications:

For the poor, "I was hungry."
For the homeless, "I was naked."
For the outsider (racial, ethnic, sexual?), "I was a stranger."
For health care, "I was sick."
For inefficient, inadequate criminal justice, "I was in prison."

All this raises the question for us: Where is the passion and identification of the American people?

Something to think about.

QUESTIONS FOR THOUGHT AND DISCUSSION

1. How would you describe what is wrong in our society?

2. How do you relate to economic determinism?

3. How do you respond to election results?

4. How do you understand prevailing negativity about our government?

5. With what portions of Jesus's society does he identify?

CHAPTER 10

About The Future

Our modern age has harnessed tremendous powers in the splitting of the atom. With the Cold War, civilization was on trial. Would we be able to utilize these powers without destroying ourselves in the process? The Cold War is over, but dangers remain. Nuclear accidents continue as a possibility. Nuclear power plants are getting older and embrittlement is affecting the structures; and we do not know what to do with all that nuclear waste. Civilization is still on trial.

Not only nuclear power, microbiology has led us to breaking the genetic code and forging into genetic engineering. We are not sure what dangers face us in genetic manipulation and altering life processes. New strains of life forms? Uncontrollable viruses? Civilization is like a bus traveling into the future. Previously we thought that the bus was being controlled. Now we seem to be racing down a hill, and, horror of horrors, no one is in the driver's seat. We are the terrified occupants anticipating a crash and trying to endure a future that has not yet arrived. Isn't this the appeal of fortune tellers and the soothsayers of our day?

Yet, a catastrophe in the near future is not inevitable. The future is in our hands, placed there by the Reality that called us into being. We can make a difference. You and I can make a difference! Something to think about.

The future looms ahead filled with unknown and yet anticipated dangers and catastrophes. But we are not pawns like the word of that fatalist poet, Omar Khayyam:

"For in and out, above, about, below,
'Tis nothing but a Magic Shadow-show,
Play'd in a Box whose Candle is the Sun,
Round which we Phantom Figures come and go."[1]

Not so. We are participants in decision-making. We can raise the question of values. We do not have to do whatever is possible without raising the question, "Why?"

A derelict-appearing man on a train was approached by a conductor who roused him for a ticket. The disheveled traveler pulled out a roll of bills and in a stupor said, "Give me a ticket to wherever it is." This little drama unnerved the author Loren Eiseley who witnessed the event and reflected on it. We face the terror of an open-ended universe. Who is able to declare a destination? We can do no better than to turn to the lonely man of Nazareth and "hear" him speak of the Kingdom of God, a kingdom where compassion and caring are the dominant forces and the unity of humanity on planet earth is recognized. Any one of us can live with the motivation of this destiny, and experience the transformation of life. Is there a better goal?

Something to think about.

---

1. *Op Cit., page 34*

The ancients used to speak of the wheel of existence. This presupposed a cyclical view of history: what has been, is, and will be. With Jesus of Nazareth a new concept of history came into focus. Not a circle but a straight line! He said, "I know where I am going." Individual lives as well as human life has a destiny, a purpose. Jesus called it the kingdom of God.

Matthew's Gospel speaks about an earthquake concurrent with the crucifixion. His metaphor was true to what has been experienced. Calvary has shaken the world. The cyclical view of history of Oriental and Greek thought has given way to a linear view of history. There was a beginning and there will be an end. The drama of one man's life is the drama of every life.

The question for us individually and corporately is: Where are we going? We are becoming but what? Self examination and self knowledge is the beginning of coming to terms with where we are going as a society. It is time for us to know our powers and our gifts and to use them to make a difference in other lives and in the natural world. This is our unique role: responsibility and opportunity.

Something to think about.

Environment and the natural world are much in the news these days. Some see the world as given to us to use as we see fit in order to gain the highest standard of living. Others, called environmentalists, see the natural world as a precious trust to be cared for and preserved for those yet unborn. We can go even farther. The natural world is a manifestation of divinity; it is the second book of revelation. Indeed, Jesus so viewed the world about him: "Look at the birds of the air . . ." "Consider the lilies of the field . . ." "A sower went out to sow his seed . . ."

So the Divine can be seen today. Remember the Osprey. Their number was being depleted and they were approaching the endangered species list. Scientists discovered that the Osprey egg shells were so thin that the eggs were being crushed in incubation. The reason? DDT! After the outlawing of this insecticide, the Osprey began a slow recovery. They gave us a signal. If we had not responded, human life would next be at risk. Some reality did not want that to happen. Shakespeare was right: "There's a divinity that shapes our ends, Roughhew them how we will."

The Divine in the natural world! Nothing provable but an exciting possibility that unites all forms of life. The animals have a right to be here, to be protected. In protecting them, we may also be protecting ourselves.

Something to think about.

Evolution? Of course! We were not created by fiat, zapped into being in one moment of time. All the evidence points to a long development of life on planet earth. Those who think otherwise are letting their theological perspective govern their rational thinking. Evolution is part of the unfolding future. What is humanity becoming? Not super-humans in the physical sense. We protect and nourish even the weak among us. In the human development of compassion, we are finding a different form of evolution — the development of spirit. We are still in the molten stage of becoming.

Jesus saw himself on a journey. Not a physical trek but an inward journey higher and more dangerous. Heaven is out there as the culmination but heaven is not a place but a state of being. Trying to make heaven objective and outward destroys its meaning. An ancient unknown saint, the author of *The Cloud of Unknowing*, wrote: "Heaven ghostly is as high down as up, and up as down; behind as before, before as behind, on one side as another. Insomuch, that whoso had a true desire for to be at heaven, then that same time he were in heaven ghostly. For the high and the next way thither is run by desires and not by paces of feet." Change ghostly to spiritually and comprehend the meaning. Heaven is a spiritual and not a physical term. It is as high down as up, and as up as down; behind as before and before as behind, on one side as another. Insomuch that whoso had a true desire for to be in heaven, then that one is already in heaven aware of the di-mensions of the spirit. The way to heaven is found not in physical terms but in terms of inward desire.

Something to think about.

The physical stuff of this universe is, as I understand it, a given. The basic elements remain the basic elements. However that mysterious power we call God brought this universe into being and however long that process took, we remain the debtors. Change will occur. We will grow better tomatoes but human beings will not likely develop into super humans. The evolution of humanity has had a remarkable development. Some of us have found compassion. No longer the survival of the fittest. Instead the development of the spirit, a new kind of humanity. In the growth of the spirit "it does not yet appear what we shall be."

Christianity is future oriented which captures that within us yearning for development and fulfillment. The future is contained within ourselves; it will emerge out of what we are today. Whatever is evil or good about the future has its seeds in us now. We do not need fortune tellers, people who misuse biblical prophecy, or who believe that the future is already predetermined. The future is emerging from now. Will it be endurable? Only if what is born comes out of compassion, out of an inner seeing of the connectedness of all things. Those who are not buried in the past but who build on it and are willing to accept change and newness of life, will have a part in that peaceable kingdom. This is the work of the Spirit.

Yes, there is One who makes all things new, a new heaven and a new earth. Not the old heaven up there, not the old concept of an earth to be raped for the benefit of a few; but a heaven and earth united in the kingdom of God, a kingdom within us, between us, and among us. I would like to have a part in that. Wouldn't you?

Something to think about.

How many of us fear the future? Ever emerging dangers threaten us. We do not know what is going to happen next.

What catastrophes await us? What tragedies will invade our life story? Objective realities will not always be to our liking. Yet objective realities need not be the factors that determine our mental and emotional state. In the process of evolution, objective reality has been replaced by subjective: the development of soul. Whatever we mean by soul, the word points to what connects us to all living things and to eternity.

John Donne had some insight into soul: ". . . any man's death diminishes me, because I am involved in Mankind . . ." We are discovering too a spiritual dimension in our relationship with plants and animals. Good music produced by humans can have a positive effect on plant life. See the film Andre (which is based on a true story) and you will discover a depth connectedness to the animal kingdom. What does all this mean?

Our human future at its best is not in the development of technology but the expansion of spirit or soul. The obsession with more advanced cars, planes, space vehicles and the like may lead to intellectual impoverishment and spiritual deadness. Our inner world is in jeopardy. It is time to look at the artist, the poet and the dramatist and discover where more and more and faster and faster are taking us. Heaven and hell are newly emerging as parts of our inner life. I cautiously suggest that heaven is related to spirit or soul and hell is that state with soul's absence.

Something to think about.

1. How secure is our future personally or socially?

2. How are we participants in social and political decision-making?

3. What is the meaning of a linear view of history?

4. What can we learn from what is happening in nature?

5. What is heaven for you?

6. What does it mean to be future oriented?

7. How do you understand evolution?

8. Can evolution be part of spiritual development?

CHAPTER 11

About Relationships

Sometime ago, we saw the movie *Shadowlands*. What a powerful and deeply moving film. The impact is due to the reality factor. Life is not romanticized but faced honestly with its polarity of deep joy and heart-rending grief. Although not accustomed to recommending films, I cannot refrain from urging mature adults to see this movie. Your conversation as well as your most intimate relationship will have an added depth dimension.

This film is about a portion of the life of C. S. Lewis. An early production features Joss Ackland and Claire Bloom. In the later version, Anthony Hopkins played C. S. Lewis. The first film is available but the Hopkins film is hard to find and is expensive.

Anyone seeing this art work will be forced to face the passingness of life and, in the process, relate more honestly to the way life is. In succeeding pages I shall attempt to reflect on: (1) the role of sickness, pain, and death in life; (2) the risk but also the joy of loving deeply; (3) the lack of simple or pietistic answers to suffering; and (4) the religious dimension in facing suffering and death.

As you have opportunity, see one of these films and then relate to my reflections with your own dialogue on the issues raised. I guarantee that you will have—

Something to think about.

I am continuing my reflections after seeing the film, *Shadowlands*. Loving another deeply is a risky venture. In loving we magnify the possibility of pain and suffering. In a love relationship we share in another's agonies. At times this becomes more excruciating than our own personal sufferings.

In a depth relationship we are always facing the possibility of loss. We become anxious about the future, anticipate that time of separation, and may even try to distance ourselves from the relationship to ease the future hurt. However, *Shadowlands* reveals another aspect of a love relationship: the possibility of happiness and joy that comes only when we enter the life of another with commitment and dedication. In such a relationship the pain of future separation is part of the happiness now, which is a near quote from the film.

Shadowlands tells us that loving is risky but that the risk is worth it. An old adage puts it well: "Better to have loved and lost than never to have loved at all."

Something to think about.

In an honest and straightforward way the movie, (*Shadowlands*), struggles with life's griefs, losses, pains, and separations in the context of the beauties of life and love. Because of the likelihood of suffering, we are tempted to choose the way of safety. Don't get involved! Keep yourself from loving too deeply! Don't share the fears and anxieties of life! Keep yourself above the ambiguities of life with a facade of security and certainty. All these efforts mask a deep loneliness.

The problem with such attempts to escape pain is that we are also walling ourselves off from a relationship that can partly assuage our loneliness by providing a joy that can only come from loving in a self-forgetful way. To share life fully with another, even to the point of sharing the inevitable realities of pain, suffering, and death, opens life to profound depths that can be reached in no other way.

Watch, therefore, your self-protectiveness, as I plan to watch mine. I do not want to miss the deeper dimensions of life that come from honestly facing the realities.

Something to think about.

Shadowlands, a deeply moving film, has given me much food for thought. I hope my reflections do more than probe my inner life by touching yours as well.

The film is profound in not offering simplistic answers to life's sufferings. Some religionists make an effort to provide us with certainties when there are none. Faith is not sight or certainty. Faith is the willingness to accept and work with the agenda life gives you when there is no absolute evidence that such faith is justified.

Shadowlands struggles with the issue of why God allows suffering and pain. Without an absolute answer, the film does point to suffering as part of our learning that we are dependent creatures and that all human striving, having, and loving are passing away.

Let me make a bold statement. God needs human suffering to be humanity's God. Without suffering, humanity would not need faith, trust, or any reaching out to the Mystery in awe of the way life is. Without suffering life would be prosaic and boring. With suffering without God, the response to life would be, at its worst, cynicism, or, at its best, stoicism—resignation to the inevitable. With some concept of God life unfolds as a struggle to find meaning in the midst of suffering and pain. In that struggle are those who discover a Presence that enables the victory of faith.

Something to think about.

In a closing scene of *Shadowlands*, father and son are sharing the emptiness that is felt when death invades personal relationships. One asks the other, "Do you believe in heaven" The other responds, "No, I don't think I do." The questioner counters, "I do, I want so much to see her again."

What a natural desire in facing the loss of a loved one. Yet, heaven is not an object of faith. Only God is. Some concept of heaven can be a part of Christian hope and Christians will differ in their response to the concept. In spite of those who want to quote Bible verses to prove heaven is a place, heaven is not provable.

Yes, the gospel of John has Jesus say that he goes to prepare a place. I don't think this is a geographical statement. This word is affirming that there is an at-home-ness about death.

Perhaps the best that we can say is that heaven is a state of being that we can share in now. What that means for after death we can only surmise. Faith simply assures us that nothing can separate us from the love of God. That non-separation is heaven and gives us the courage to face life's sufferings and deaths. We might wish for more than this, but I think that faith in that One Final Reality is enough.

Something to think about.

QUESTIONS FOR THOUGHT AND DISCUSSION

1. Who has seen "*Shadowlands*?" If you are in a group, suggest that those who have talk about it.

2. In loving we magnify the possibilities of pain and suffering. Can you talk about such experiences?

3. Can you share experiences of trying to escape pain and suffering by not loving?

4. Is it possible that God needs suffering? What would it mean to believe that God needs human suffering to be our God?

5. How does faith cope with suffering?

CHAPTER 12

About Perfection

"Be perfect as your Heavenly Father is perfect," so we are admonished in the Sermon on the Mount. But what does this mean? Is this physical or relational perfection? I don't think so. Such a drive for perfection is superficial and can be very destructive.

Who wants to be related to a perfectionist? Such a person is not easy to live with. Perfectionism is a disease that infects one with a desire to return to some pristine condition or to graduate to some future state removed from errors and shortcomings. Such people are intolerant of the weaknesses in the rest of us and often oblivious to their own failings.

We need, I think, the courage of imperfection. This means trusting our creation. Beauty and imperfection go together. Every tree is less than perfect. Some have very obvious scars from injuries past. Every human body has blemishes. And each of us is in a state of deterioration. Relationally we continue to say things we ought not say and do things we should not do.

Whatever being perfect means, it is not physical and relational perfection. The drive for such perfection may only serve to separate us from one another. Something more needs to be said and will be next.

Something to think about.

What does it mean to be perfect? Obviously we are not perfect in a physical or relational sense. We are deteriorating, dying! Is that going on to perfection? A rabbi and a young boy were walking and came across a dead bird. The boy asked the rabbi, "Why do birds die? Why does anything die?" The rabbi responded, "The Great Rabbi wanted life to be precious. Something that is yours forever is never precious." So we live with death and dying and in the process recognize how precious life is.

Our relational flaws are of like nature. If we never said or did anything out of order, we would not need forgiveness or understanding. Because we are not relationally perfect means that we must rely on others to accept us as we are, and to relate to us in spite of. This necessity produces depth of relationships not possible, I think, if we were relationally perfect.

Each of us has physical and relational scars. Grand Canyon has nothing on us. Can we celebrate the scars with which we are deeply and delicately scored? Our imperfections serve to unite us and lead us to assist one another. What, therefore, being perfect means awaits treatment.

Something to think about.

The Sermon on the Mount tells us to be perfect as our Heavenly Father is perfect. We have been saying that this does not mean physical or relational perfection. In the kind of world given us, this is not possible. A deeper meaning to perfection is discovered by the context in which the term is used. The perfection is in love, in non-calculating, self-giving love. This love is not simply loving those who love you; it is a love that reaches out in good-will even to those who appear unlovable.

Being perfect as God is perfect is being complete and whole in compassionate and caring love. No one of us is going to be perfect in insight, free from mistakes, or so independent that we need no one. John Wesley asked all his preachers if they were going on to perfection. If that is not the object, what is? Shall we set our goal on imperfection in love? Life offers us the possibility, by virtue of the love by which we are loved, to reach out far and near in compassion, caring love, and depth of concern. Nothing less is demanded of us and nothing more is possible given our physical frailties and relational weaknesses. We have not arrived yet, but we press on to that high calling that we see exemplified in the Man of Nazareth.

Something to think about.

QUESTIONS FOR THOUGHT AND DISCUSSION

1. What does perfection mean to you?

2. Does perfection mean there is no need for improvement?

3. Does perfection in love mean more to you than the elusive perfectionism?

CHAPTER 13

About Words

Elections are much in the news. This is the time when the words liberal and conservative are bandied about. But what do the terms mean? Can we get beyond the pejorative stereotypes to understand what liberalism and conservatism are all about?

Liberalism is the belief in the consistent and comprehensive improvement of society. The real liberal works for change but, at the same time, sees no weakness in accepting the good faith of those who disagree with some proposed change. The true liberal also feels no disgrace in admitting that a held opinion may be wrong.

The conservative stands for stability as opposed to innovation, restraint instead of daring, preservation of inherited conditions as opposed to drastic reforms. True conservatives are opposed to liberalism but not destructive of it.

Liberals and conservatives are in both religion and politics, and usually, but not always, what you are in one you are in the other. Both conservatives and liberals have essential roles in our society. They are the twin structural supports of constitutional government. Either, however, can be distorted or corrupted. Unfortunately, this is what seems to happen around every election.

Something to think about.

Good and evil are polar opposite words. How do we use them? Sometimes it seems that we are motivated more by perceived evil than we are by love of the good. Many are more adept in expressing what they are against than what they are for. The hatred of evil boils up like steam and becomes pathological unless moderated by the love of good.

Goodness is real and has some obvious contrasts with evil. Let me suggest some characteristics of the good, which I admit are personal opinions. Dialogue is good while opinionated rigidity is evil. Some are so sure they are right that they refuse really to listen to anything opposite. "Don't bother me with your opinions; I have already made up my mind." Respect for different opinions is good while castigating any opinion but one's own is evil. Election periods are when those of political extremes refuse to see any validity in the opposition. Religious disagreements are of like nature. How hard it is to put on the shoes of another and try to imagine the others' concerns.

An openness to learn from others is good while suspicion of the opinions and motivation of others is evil. True, there are some opinions that are so evil, so inhumane, that they lead to revulsion. But basically Democrats and Republicans are not so separated and neither are Methodists and Baptists, to use two among many examples. The "we" approach to politics and religion has much to commend it. The "they" approach leads to no listening and no learning. In the process, all suffer.

Something to think about.

Religious writings sometimes refer to Satan. What is the term? What or who is Satan? What are we to think of Satan? The term means "adversary" and refers to that which stands in opposition to God's purposes for humanity. It is the personification of evil.

The use of the term "Satan" is only found three times in the Jewish Scriptures and these are all post-exilic (after the Babylonian captivity of the Jews). This shows the influence of Zoroastrianism which had Ahriman (also called Shaitin) as the god of evil. After the exile Satan became a personalized being. Before this "satan" or "adversary" was used to refer to the enemy of Saul, Hadad, or even David. After the exile, the culture was replete with mythological figures and Satan became one of them. No one raised the question about the real existence of such figures. The truth is that the adversary to God's purposes is that which opposes reconciliation and the unity of humanity. This is the evil, the absence of good, that is symbolized by Satan.

Christians today, not understanding the nature of mythology, can easily make the mistake of objectifying Satan and confusing the issue of evil in the world. Jesus and the New Testament writers, especially the author of Revelation, used mythology to get at the truth about the power of evil with other than philosophical discourse. God is the author of a creation in process. Chaos is the opposition to that process. Chaos, nothingness, is the adversary to God that threatens us all. That is what Satan means to many of us. Do we need more?

Something to think about.

The pursuit of happiness is the driving force in many lives. But the more we search for happiness the more it seems to elude us. We try to find happiness in pleasure, but no pleasure lasts to give us happiness. We think that happiness is supposed to be in family life. The complexities and difficulties in most families mean that happiness is not the product of family relationships. In desperation we attempt to find happiness by working to manage our children, mate, or some other. In the process we lose self in the effort to control the people in our lives.

Happiness can never be a permanent state in our kind of world. Perhaps all we can expect are some fleeting moments here and there. But joy is something else. Joy comes to those who sense their participation in the very purposes of God. Joy is the satisfaction that comes from being alive and having the resources needed to meet the issues of life. Joy is knowing that one is loved no matter what. Joy is, therefore, the product of God's love which is not earned; it is a gift.

Something to think about.

Some Christians take delight in using the phrase "born again." They take pride in thinking of themselves as born again Christians. Where did this phrase come from? The Gospel of John! Where did the author of the Gospel of John get this term? From Greek mystery religions! Mithraism was one of the main competitors of Christianity and was the official cult of the Roman Empire at the end of the third century. According to a Persian myth, Mithras was the youthful god of light who killed a sacred bull, from whose blood and semen new life was generated. Only men were initiated into this religion and after the ceremony followers were said to have been born again. They lived from then on, according to Mithraism, under the god's special protection.

John and First Peter are the only places where this phrase is found, though the term "born of the Spirit" is found in other letters. "Born again" is borrowed language to communicate the experience that early Christians had of newness of life. Indeed the image is useful when not used to separate Christians. We are born turned inward. We are reborn turned outward to consider the needs of the neighbor and not just our own. This has validity, but to use "born again" to separate Christians is both a prideful and an arrogant practice not worthy of followers of Jesus.

Something to think about.

Salvation—an old word! What does it mean? Salvation is both from something and for something. Like one rescued from drowning, salvation is from death and for life. Death takes many forms: fear, frustration, hatred, guilt, despair. To be saved is to be set free from the destructive effects of these negative states. To be saved is to be healed, to be made whole.

When one experiences salvation, one can deal with the negatives in life with faith, hope and love. A saved life is made possible by the awareness that no matter what, life is undergirded by accepting and affirming love. The gift of love is a free gift. The source of that love is a mystery which some choose to call God.

The question, "Are you saved?" does not involve using the right words but experiencing the rightness of being alive and being loved. That love enables us to love both self and others which, in essence, is wholeness of life. This in essence is salvation.

Something to think about.

What is the Christian faith in a nutshell? Crucifixion and resurrection! Old words but don't tune them out!

Crucifixion says that fullness of life involves suffering. Suffering takes many forms. Sometimes we are misunderstood or face loneliness. At other times we suffer the physical pain of sickness or the agony of grief. These are not crucifixions but the inevitable consequences of life. Crucifixion is a voluntary identification with the sufferings of others to the point of self-giving love. Such was Jesus' life and so it can be with us. We die to self and assume some responsibility for others.

But this is not all. Crucifixion is not the last word. Whatever the negativities of life, the sharing in death-like experiences, they are not the full story. Resurrection emerges just one step past crucifixion. Resurrection is newness of life with possibilities for the present and hope for the future.

Crucifixion is not sought for itself. Unless we are mentally sick, we do not choose to be crucified. But sometimes the cross is the inevitable consequence of self-giving love, the projecting of ourselves into the lives of others. And resurrection is not what is expected. When it comes we know it to be a gift of God.

Something to think about.

---

1. k~11j

Words are fascinating. Some stimulate our curiosity. Others make us feel uncomfortable. Sin is one of the latter words; but try as we might, we cannot seem to get rid of the term. We know that the word points to realities in our lives.

What is sin? Try this for a definition: Sin is a state of being which results in a strained and/or destructive relationship with oneself, others, or the created order. This means that sin does not necessarily involve bad acts or illegal activities. All of us are involved in sin. For some this may mean immoral acts, but most of us find socially acceptable ways of sinning. When we are separated relationally from family or friends, that is sin. When we are uncaring in relation to human need, that is sin. When we are in deep depression and hate our life, we all need healing, wholeness, and forgiveness – not once and for all but again and again. Thanks be to God that this is exactly what is offered to us. Forgiveness given calls for gratitude. Gratitude in turn leads us to do something about separation and uncaring. It may mean getting help.

Something to think about.

QUESTIONS FOR THOUGHT AND DISCUSSION

1. If you define yourself as a conservative what does that mean? If liberal, do the same.

2. How would you contrast good and evil?

3. What do you believe about Satan?

4. What does it mean to be happy?

5. What does the phrase "born again" mean to you?

6. What does the term "salvation" mean to you?

7. How, if ever, do you use the word "sin"?

CHAPTER 14

About Writing

Wholeness of life can be advanced by writing because writing encourages thought and reflection. Too often we go from experience to experience, event to event, person to person without ever pausing to reflect on what is happening to us. Paper and pen (or pencil) help us stop in the rush of life to be present to what is going on, to (in a sense) take life in. Let me be confessional here. Writing has not come easy for me. I am an activist doer. But for forty or more years my profession has called on me to write. I have been forced to express myself and to reflect on my life and the world around me. This has been a blessing.

I am here urging you, whatever your work, to write. I am convinced that writing is both health and wholeness producing. Whatever clarity of thought I have has come from writing. Some can and do raise some question about that clarity; but I shudder to think about what my life would be without the discipline of writing. Whatever probing I have done into the depths of my own life is the result of the thought and reflection brought on by writing. This leads me to rejoice at the opportunity of writing these pages. You too can be blessed by writing. Why not try something more than the occasional letter? You may be surprised.

Something to think about.

What more than shallow, horizontal living does life offer us? Each of us has an outward life. This consists of experiences, events, and a constant flow of people. Each of us can also have an inward life involving thought, reflection and meditation. The first is automatic; the second is up to us. The key to wholeness of life is a balance between the inward and outward dimensions of life.

An inward life takes some effort and discipline. One of the best ways to develop such a life is writing. Writing encourages thought and reflection. Humanity's greatest attribute is perhaps the ability to communicate. Oral communication was a giant step forward in human evolution, but the written word gave the boost that bought culture with all its manifold aspects. Writing helps the writer to develop the inner life. Writing is one means of communicating with oneself, clarifying thinking and processing experiences.

The result is greater emotional health. Why not try keeping a journal? If you do not daily, at least write after those kairos moments of deep meaning. You may be surprised at the enrichment of life that writing provides.

Something to think about.

I have been urging you to write. Your health and well-being may be improved by so doing. The possibilities are varied. The most intensive and disciplined way of journaling is using the Progoff method of The Intensive Journal or <u>The Practice of Process Meditation</u>. His workshops, some years ago, or those done by certified leaders, were held over the country. People who participated in this method are excited about what it does for them. Progoff's books were best sellers.

Again, let me be confessional. I have not been to a workshop and do not use his method of disciplining my writing. I am more spasmotic and situational in recording my thoughts and reflections. But I have a friend who uses this method, and I asked her to give me a few words about her experience. She said that journaling was for her a means of centering, of getting perspective—re-aligning, focusing, remembering what is important and what's ahead. Her writing, she reported, is a way of moving on or through. "When I am stuck, I can write out all the aspects that I am conscious of—even a dialogue with a person or experience—and then push it aside. Journal writing is a way of taking my inner life seriously, even in a meeting when temporarily I turn into myself in the midst of others to get perspective."

On the next page I want to share with you my paper pondering after I developed "floaters." This just may give you—

Something to think about.

Writing about my experiences provides a compass and enables me to orient my life and get positioned in a new direction. A number of years ago I developed "floaters" in my eyes. After my session with the ophthalmologist, I sat down and wrote the following:

Why my eye? Is this what it means to be growing old? The breaking away of the vitreous jell is what the doctor called it. A floater is the designation. This means that I am always seeing things off to the side, like cobwebs. Sometimes, without thinking, I try to brush it away. Disconcerting!

Well, it has happened, I cannot make it unhappen. What do I do about it? Accept it? Yes, but not without some protest. The doctor said, "To be safe, don't run for a few weeks." But I was a jogger. That's not what I want. Can good come out of this situation? Well, yes! Before I ran and Frances (my wife) walked. Now we walk together. We have an additional thirty minutes of conversation time and that is good. And the walking is just as good as running if you extend the time a bit. More than this, I am learning to appreciate my eyesight. What a precious gift! To be able to see, cobwebs and all, is an amazing ability. Besides, I am discovering that little by little I do not notice the floaters, except when I decide to see If they are still there. When I check, I discover that they are.

Why not try writing about your life experiences. You may discover a new part of yourself.

Something to think about.

Here is one more bit in my attempt to inspire you to write. This piece has a sad, melancholy tone to it. But is anyone not there at times? To understand this you need to know that a gopher once tunneled up to my foot, a hummingbird once perched on my thumb, and Cluster Oaks is a vacation place we have at Canyon Lake, Texas.

As a self-conscious creature I am aware of being separate and distinct from others and that fact isolates me. I think and that turns me within. I feel and that makes me even more self-aware. Yet, at times, that thinking and feeling have an outward movement. I think about what is out there that is separate from me. I feel about some scene, animal, or person in the process of trying to take in some experience.

How do I explain my emotions in relation to the gopher, the hummingbird, the waterfall, or Cluster Oaks? Are we all part of that same primordial dust so that though separate we share in some essence? (God in everything and everything in God?) But the mystery is that humans are aware of this connection; matter is not. When I see Cluster Oaks for the last time, if I am aware of that, I shall be sad (like Paul Tillich about South Hampton); but Cluster Oaks will continue to be oblivious to me. There is something unfair about that. I think I would like to make some difference to that place — to be missed.

What is this wanting to be remembered, wanting to be missed? I want to count for something and to make a difference in this world, I cannot see simply being as sufficient; it is doing, relating, initiating, growing that gives uniqueness. So I shall continue to spend myself in all the doing — my constant effort to make a difference, which in the end will fail to accomplish what I deeply desire."

Perhaps these last pages are too personal, but I really want readers to become writers as well.

Something to think about.

You who read this also write. You know the demand of a blank sheet of paper that needs to be transformed into an article or a letter. Think how strange it is that we make squiggly lines on a piece of paper and someone else can see and hear: "I love you." "Forgive me." "I should like to see you." "I'm sorry."

So in ancient Sumer a person seeing bird prints in the hardened clay must have thought that such prints could be arranged to communicate. He or she did and cuneiform writing was born. The Sumerians began writing and humanity has not been the same since.

I write in the hope that I can communicate something to you of love, joy, peace, excitement, grace, victory, thanksgiving. Do I? That's for you to say. But you too can write. You too can communicate. So write to someone.

And this is more than something to think about.

QUESTIONS FOR THOUGHT AND DISCUSSION

1. How do you feel about writing?

2. What are the barriers to your writing?

3. How often have you wanted to write something but did not discipline yourself to do so?

CHAPTER 15

About Remembering Loren Eiseley

This chapter begins a series on the writings of Loren Eiseley, my favorite author, who has profound insights into the nature of humanity. He was a boundary figure between literature and science. As a physical anthropologist, he was fascinated by the mysteriousness, illogic, and arbitrariness of the physical world and human evolution.

Early in his career he turned away from the restrictions of scientific articles to the literary forms of personal essays and poetry. His earnest desire was to express his sense of wonder and awe at nature's complexity, the human ties with the natural world, and the mystery of humanity's strange reaching out to something beyond. He became convinced that the secret of life will not yield to the kind of analysis that science is capable of producing. Instead, that secret is found deep within the human psyche and humanity's awareness that life is more than its physical manifestation.

His themes involve anti-materialism, opposition to a narrow rationalism, fascination with human physical development and genetic endowment, and wonder at the vastness of time and the manifold interlinking of humanity with all forms of life.

As we shall see, he believed in a natural revelation found in the merging of humanity and nature and especially those points at which the mundane world gives way to another dimension of life.

Something to think about.

We are in a series on the writings of Loren Eiseley who before his death was chair of the Department of Anthropology at the University of Pennsylvania. He was elected to the National Institute of Arts and Letters because of his literary skills. Eiseley was both a scientist and literary artist and, in addition, a deeply spiritual man. We are going to relate some of his experiences with nature and his probing reflections afterward.

On one of his excursions he came upon a strange sight. At a distance he saw what appeared to be a ball like object with a rope attached bouncing up and down on a rocky flat. Upon closer examination he found a hen pheasant with the coil of a king snake wrapped around its body. The issue was likely whether a clutch of eggs was going to become wings or scales. The bouncing was the pheasant trying to escape the coil. In the process the snake was being pounded on the rocks and the pheasant was rapidly losing energy. What should Eiseley do? As a scientist he could well have watched to see what would be the outcome! Instead he arbitrated the matter by unwinding the snake (non- poisonous) and removing it from the scene.

What was going on here? He reflected. The pheasant was contesting for her eggs. The snake was intent on a meal. For what was Eiseley contending? The answer came to him. As a human he could contain more than self by embracing both the bird and the snake. He was contending for a more comprehensive version of himself. He embraced both creatures by transcending feather and scale into another sphere of reality. He had become the reconciler, which was not anything he learned in science. Humans as reconcilers! That fits the Gospel message.

Something to think about.

The Star Thrower, pg. 291 ff.

Loren Eiseley was a deeply spiritual man. He reflected on human life crossing the open domain of space with various mechanical probes. I can "hear" him pondering the newest word from the Hubble telescope. By our mechanical extensions we are reaching out into sidereal space. What are we going to find? Have we come from elsewhere? Are we going to discover something not to our liking?

Eiseley entertained such thoughts as he was standing by a pond and noticed a frog. He was aware of standing still and not moving a muscle so as not to disturb the creature. Then a remarkable insight! Here is the most enormous extension of vision of which human life is capable. This is more than any space exploration. Humans can project themselves into other lives and adjust their behavior so as not to threaten or harm some other creature. As he thought about that he came to the conclusion that this was "the magnificent power of humanity," "more than any spacial adventure, the supreme epitome of reaching out."

Something to think about.

The Immense Journey, pg. 45 ff.

Loren Eiseley, about whose works we have been reflecting in these pages, became disillusioned by the religion of science. He turned aside from the rigid assumption that every natural event can be rationally explained by prior events. (He, of course, is not alone among scientists with this understanding) He affirmed: "I no longer believe that science will save the world."

Eiseley made reference to a theological work, *The Idea of the Holy* by Rudolph Otto, written years ago and still being read. This work still speaks to all who are impressed with the mysterium tremendum, which is nothing less than the awe that many feel when reflecting on human life. Such reflections Freud dismissed as being irrational. Eiseley saw two camps among scientists. One has a sense of wonder before the universal mystery that hides in the physical world. The other is the reductionist who attempts to tear everything apart until the mystery is counted as not worth bothering about.

Eiseley asserts that in science as in religion when wonder, awe, and compassion are eliminated, that which makes humans human is killed in the process, even if humans continue to go about their scientific tasks. We can be impressed today with the many scientists, like the physicist Freeman Dyson, about whom this cannot be said.

Something to think about.

The Star Thrower, pgs. 189, 190, 198

Loren Eiseley, the scientist and literary artist upon whose works we are focusing, was awed by the mystery of humanity. From whence have we come? To what purpose are we directed? To say "God" is too easy and ignores human curiosity. We are justified in saying God only after we have done the mental probing that pushes us back to the past for provisional answers. Only when we can go no farther are we justified by a faith projection.

Eiseley wonders about the rich mental life that is possible for humans. The artistic qualities are more than is needed for mere survival. Humans betray more that a physical life focused on physical needs. Our mental and spiritual life are wondrous parts of our humanity. Eiseley reflects on what had to happen for this aspect of our life to develop. First, millennia ago, the human brain had to treble in size. This had to happen after birth and not before. Next, childhood had to lengthen to allow for the brain to receive, store, and learn from others. For this to happen family bonds had to survive seasonal mating.

All this occurred in a hurry millennia ago, with each step following the other in succession. This developmental process came about in God's good time when earth was ready for this new species. How this happened and our connection with other forms of life are mysteries still lost in the past. But we are here and can be grateful for the possibilities of that rich mental life that is available to us. This is, above all, what differentiates us from the animal kingdom and leads us to reach out to comprehend that Beyond that is strangely involved in our world.

Something to think about.

We are probing further into Loren Eiseley who was a scientist understanding that science can never answer all the questions arising from our humanity. He wondered: Isn't it strange how humans escaped from the specialization of parts common to evolution? We assign to our clothing and our technology the activities for which animals had to develop organs in the body. We take off and put on; we add various gadgets to our homes; we travel by way of computer to be in touch with the rest of the world. By intellect alone we have taken from nature the power of change exerted on all other forms of life. Our minds have become more important than bodily structure.

Eiseley joined Wallace, a contemporary of Darwin, believing that Mind was behind the emergence of humanity. Natural selection alone could only have produced a savage human with a brain only a few degrees superior to that of an ape. The absence of much of bodily hair and the strange development of the human larynx mystified Wallace. But Eiseley went further to see that the emergence of love, compassion, and empathy (far exceeding anything in the natural world — whales and dolphins perhaps excepted) points beyond a physical survival of the fittest to a creature whose fullest life is found in mind and spirit. Here is the grandeur that is humanity, a grandeur not understood by any rational hypothesis but finds its grounding in something beyond.

Something to think about.

Who am I? The answer to that question is more than a name and address or any other group of statistics. With Loren Eiseley we can assert that we cannot establish our own reality. What is the life that is in me? In a wondrous piece of writing Loren Eiseley reflects on this question.

"There is no life in the carbon in my body . . . no life in the iron ... no life in the phosphorus, the nitrogen does not contain me, the water that soaks my tissues is not I. What am I then? . . . the minute I start breaking this strange body down into its constituents, it is dead . . . Carbon does not speak, calcium does not remember, iron does not weep."

Where am I? Where are you? Have you not in the lonely hours of the night asked yourself the question: "Who am I?" The answer is not in ourselves, not in any self analysis. We are a unique animal on a strange journey knowing that our identity is not in anything that we see; it is beyond us. In the words of Thomas Carlyle: "... there is an Infinite in (us), which with all our cunning (we) cannot bring under the Finite."

Something to think about.

Night Country, pg. 51 ff.

Loren Eiseley did not claim any expertise in theology. Yet he could not help but make some theological references as he pondered the mysteries of life. In *Man, Time, and Prophecy* he mentions that the wise traveler from Galilee knew where he was going. He was on a journey which was more inward than outward. Although his physical journey led to Golgotha, his spiritual journey was higher and more dangerous.

Quoting from an ancient and anonymous text under the title, *The Cloud of Unknowing*, the author moves us from heaven as a definable place to a spiritual dimension on our inward journey. "Heaven ghostly (spiritually) is as high down as up, and up as down: behind as before, before as behind, on one side as another." In other words heaven is not some place locatable but is a perpendicular aspect of life intersecting life at every point. We best know this in ecstasy experiences and moments of deep personal meaning. But heaven can also be known in the midst of grief and pain as we accept the realities of life and dare to trust that heaven is here even though we may not experience it at the moment.

Eiseley reminds us that we should not conceive bodily or literally what is meant spiritually; that even if we use bodily words like up and down, ascended and descended, in or out, we are seeing inwardly and not outwardly. How hard it is for us to see this at times and get bogged down in a mind-shackling literalism that misses the spirit or heaven.

Something to think about.

The treatment of The Cloud of Unknowing is also found earlier in this book.

Loren Eiseley writes about the loneliness that is the natural state of being human. "To the day of our deaths we exist in an inner solitude that is linked to the nature of life itself." Across the millennia inside has fought outside and inside has won the battle. Our bodily functions are, for the most part, automatic. When they do go wrong, outside destroys inside as when inside develops a high fever, cancer, or some other debilitating disease.

The price we pay for individual consciousness is loneliness. No one else can feel our sorrow; no one else can bear our pain; no other can intrude on our private thoughts. Our bodies are our own individual prisons. Yet in our most creative moments our inside roams the universe, reaching out to the stars and probing the mysteries of life. Even when our bodies are about to stop functioning, our thoughts embrace an unlimited universe.

Perhaps the most amazing aspect of our loneliness is the ability to love. We are able to extend love and affection to other lonely creatures, but, even more than that, we project an infinite love out of our finite bodies. We love life; we love being; we love the ground of all being—which is to love God. We reach out far beyond the physical universe of which we are a part and take in the wondrous mystery of a love by which we are loved. This love gives our finite selves a part of eternity. "This is a crossing beside which light-years are meaningless. It is the solitary key to the prison that is (the finite human)."

Something to think about.

The Invisible Pyramid, pg. 48

We are continuing with our probing into the writings of Loren Eiseley. Who has not wondered about human origins? The answer about beginnings has led us into controversy. Is creation by fiat or by process? Some would have us believe that anything but fiat (humans coming full-blown without evolving from other forms of life) eliminates God. Not so! We cannot confine God to our presuppositions.

Some may prefer not to think about origins, but most of us are invested with a native curiosity. That is what makes Eiseley's writings so provocative. He leads us back to the Neanderthal humans who lived some 40,000 years ago. Were they the ferocious beasts whom we would be scared to meet? But they lived and cared for other than themselves. A one armed human was buried with care, some others placed flints around the head and a haunch of meat in the grave for the unknown journey. Even then the human spirit in-cluded love and compassion. Across the centuries the word has come: We too were human; we too suffered; we too had beliefs; we too loved.

Somewhere in the distant past, light came into the dark world and humanity has not been the same since. We ceased evolving as physical creatures with the development of love and compassion. This remains as the unique human characteristic in spite of the inhumanity we see with crime, terrorism, and ethnic cleansing.

Something to think about.

The Firmament of Time, pg. 144

The scientist and literary artist, Loren Eiseley, gives us much food for thought. In one of his scientific works he refers to humans suffering for what they are and hungering to be otherwise. Who does not want to be something more, to experience some growth toward an elusive fulfillment? A human characteristic is a longing to be different.

Long ago a primitive people left paintings on cave walls. I have seen some of these in a cave near Abique, New Mexico. They left signs of their existence and their reaching out for understanding of themselves and their world. Are we any different? Today we write books, diaries, and journals; and we make entries on our computers in an attempt to leave something by which to be remembered. Our reaching out for something more than our present existence is part of the spiritual evolution of humanity. When we fail to wish to be different, to long for a fulfillment not yet realized, we will cease to evolve. We humans are on a journey and each step moves us into a future that will be different from the past. Our hope is that this movement will be a positive improvement and not a deterioration.

Something to think about.

Darwin and the Mysterious Mr. X, pg. 233

Is there something beyond the world that we know? An experience with a yellow and black orb spider led Loren Eiseley to reflect on such a question. He came across the spider in an arroyo. Here was the spider's universe with its senses confined to the lines and spokes of the great web it inhabited. Eiseley took a pencil from his pocket and touched a strand of the web. An immediate response led the web to vibrate until it was a blur. Any insect would have been entrapped. But the pencil point was an intrusion without precedent. "Spider was circumscribed by spider ideas; its universe was spider universe. All outside was irrational, extraneous . . . I realized that in the world of spider I did not exist."

Eiseley saw the spider as the human in miniature. We too lie at the heart of a web. "Our lines reach out into space, into the dark of pre-history, and also into the nucleus of the atom with the electron microscope. This is a new web which never existed before. We are at the heart of it listening; but we are also restricted. What is beyond our lines that we do not see? Are we part of something not amenable to our physical senses? As humans we are gifted with an awareness not native to the spider. We wonder at the beyond. We reflect on the Mystery of "the ultimate Dreamer, who dreamed the light and the galaxies." Like the spider, we too wait for some information, some indication of a movement into our world. Unlike the spider, many of us sense that there is some reality beyond the lines which we have extended into our spaces.

Something to think about.

The Unexpected Universe, pg. 49 ff

How gratifying it is to find a scientist who is aware of the limitations of science. Loren Eiseley sees experimental science restricting truth and reality to empirical limits. But authoritarian science is just as faulty as authoritarian religion. Description and analysis alone cannot provide a full understanding of the natural world. When human understanding exists only in the light of reason, we may say with certainty that the most unique aspect of humanity will be gone.

We have assigned to science, which is a human intellectual invention, a role of omnipotence not inherent in the invention. Our itch for absolute knowledge and power will forever elude us. We need a growth of human responsibility adequate to control the powers that science has put into our hands. Science may abstract its theories from reality but does not have the power to dominate or control it. Eiseley sees intuition (or a spiritual sensitivity), as part of the humanities, a surer guide to the future than the prognostications of science.

A world of the spirit, for lack of a better term, is open to humans.

Process theology holds that God is self-limited in God's omnipotence but not in love and compassion. That spirit dimension is part of humanity at its best. And even as we suffer with the suffering, may it not be that God may move with us in similar pain up the dark roads of the human journey?

Something to think about.

We must come to a conclusion of these thoughts stimulated by the scientist/literary artist, Loren Eiseley. In his writings he makes science an intensely personal and often mystical experience. The subjective and illusive dimensions of the natural world lead him to ponder the Mysterious Other behind it all.

As we have seen, Eiseley has an intense love for the small and often lost ones of this world: things beaten on the surf, birds singing and falling; the dog that dies, the baby fox still innocent. W. H. Auden wrote that Eiseley was trained in the habit of prayer by which he meant in the habit of listening open to the Word, the Spirit. Both Eiseley and Thoreau believed that the highest mark of civilization is not technical mastery but the culture's ability to live in harmony with its surroundings and not destroying what it enjoys. Nature is to be more admired than used. Some of the anti-environmentalists need to hear this word.

So I commend to you the fifteen or sixteen books of Loren Eiseley for your enlightenment and inspiration. He was a religious man in the deepest sense. His own words say it: "I who profess no religion, find that my whole life has been a religious quest."

Something to think about.

NO QUESTIONS BUT SUGGESTIONS

If a solitary individual is reading this book, reflect on Loren Eiseley's insights. Perhaps you can talk about some pages with a family member or friend.

If a class is using this book, hopefully all can read this chapter and discuss in class what was most meaningful.

CHAPTER 16

About Advent and Christmas

Advent in the Christian Year is a time for watching and waiting but not in a state of passivity. When waiting is passive, we get more and more anxious. We have ourselves on our hands and tend to fret and fume over unfulfilled expectations. But when waiting is active, when we are in a state of preparation for whatever is coming, we have the joy of involvement, the satisfaction in participating in that which is to come.

As it is with Christmas, so with life. Thornton Wilder's Emily in "Our Town" and Robin William's character in "Dead Poets Society" look at the preciousness of every day from two different perspectives. Emily, back momentarily from the dead, mourns the lack of her family's being actively present to one another. Williams' teacher wants his students to explore life and not let it pass by.

Advent is watching and waiting in the midst of daily chores, the busy schedules; being present to the people in our lives; and preparing for the love and good will that is even now ready for a greater advent into life.

Something to think about.

Advent is the season in the Church Year to accent hope. In the words of Paul: "The God of hope fill you with all joy and peace in believing that by the power of the Holy Spirit you may abound in hope." Hope is one of the main elements of the Christian faith. This hope is not for something specific that we want for ourselves: a few thousand dollars, a return of health, a new relationship, fame or fortune. Christian hope is in the activity of God working for reconciliation, harmony, and good will in the human community.

One author has expressed it: "What oxygen is for the lungs, such is hope for the meaning of life." Those who hope already have psychic energy directed towards a future that builds on and improves the present. In hope the future enters us and transforms itself in us long before it comes to pass. We are different because whatever the situation, the present is not the last word.

Something to think about.

Christmas is coming. The word is peace and good will among all people. We have less than that. We are afraid of people who are different from us. We are suspicious of non-conformists. In spite of all the evidence of reduced tensions, we continue to arm ourselves as well as serve as arms merchant for the world. We say we want a balance of power in the world but we supply arms to regimes that use those arms against their own people. More weapons! More destructive capacity! More inhumanity! When will it stop?

The same God who loves us loves the others. The same Lord offers peace and good will to all. Instead of expecting the worst and planning for it (a sure way to assure the worst coming), perhaps it is time to expect something positive and constructive. Christmas is the right time to change our focus. Just as we are helping to relieve the sufferings of an earthquake, we can relate to another people giving evidence that we want fullness of life for them. Such a life is hardly compatible with more arms and greater threat to others. Our role is to work for peace and harmony through negotiated settlement of disputes. Here and there we are doing just that, but in some areas we are not. What is our vision of the future? We help to form the future by our vision of that future. The Christmas vision is peace and good will.

Something to think about.

Throughout winter's weeks of biting winds, sharp cold spells, frequent frosts, and perhaps even a rare snowfall, the human heart is reflective. Before a warm fireplace or a welcome stove, we raise our questions about life. What is it all about? What is life's meaning and purpose? Who am I?

Even as we think of Christmas trees and house decorations, we search for answers. In winter the heart seeks its identity and longs for some revelations. Seldom do we get answers. But we do get some intimations in the family circle, in the warmth of our homes, and in the depths of our hearts. Christmas has its way of speaking to us in spite of all the trappings. What we "hear" is that even as we seek we have been found. In spite of ourselves, love has found us, and life is good.

Something to think about.

How could we manage without signs: street signs, directional signs, route signs? At the Christmas season, signs are all around us. The aged Simeon said of the child Jesus that he was given for a sign. Matthew proclaims that Jesus was the long-expected one, the fulfillment of a sign. Now we are surrounded by signs.

The babe in a manger is a sign of newness of life. The lights on our streets and homes are signs that light has come into the world's darkness. Wrapped packages are signs of love. Representations of angels are signs of the message of peace and good will. Even Santa Claus is a sign of benevolence and harkens back to St. Nicholas, Bishop of Myra in the 4th century, who, among other things, gave gifts to children.

How can we live without signs? In spite of the excesses, again and again one or another of the Christmas signs gives me courage and hope. How about you?

Something to think about.

Stories often have imbedded in them profound truths that illuminate life. Being factual or historical is not necessary for a story to reveal meaningful truth. So it is with an ancient tale recorded by Jonas Mekas, editor of *Film Culture*. The story: Adam and Eve were leaving the Garden of Eden and Adam fell asleep in the shadow of a rock. Eve looked back toward Eden and saw the globe of Paradise exploding into millions of bits and fragments. Then the fragments of Paradise rained into the souls of Eve and the sleeping Adam.

What are the fragments of Paradise if not the ecstatic, the creative explosions in human life? All forms of art (like poems, drama, stories, music, and painting), are those bits of Paradise reflected in human life. In spite of many forms of inhumanity and the sordidness in many relationships, the fragments are present. Here and there they get expressed to make more noble human life and to give us a glimpse of that Paradise that has been part of the human journey.

Christmas is one of the times when those fragments are revealed to those who have eyes to see and ears to hear.

Something to think about.

Various forms of art are fragments of Paradise in human life. The previous page offered this perspective emerging from an old tale about Adam and Eve. Story-telling has its origins in an ancient way of expressing truths too deep for facts. So it is with the stories of Christmas that are not history but art forms.

The Christmas stories of an announcing angel, a manger, shepherds in the fields, angelic chorus, and wise men from the East all speak of truths that are more than facticity. What are these truths? God is more likely to come to us in the humble and lowly than in the high and mighty (Joseph, Mary, and a cattle stall). God meets us in our ordinary tasks not primarily in formal religious activity (shepherds in a field). The revelation of God has cosmic significance (star and angels).

At Christmas we read and tell these stories not because they are facts (though some choose to claim that they are) but because they speak truths to a deeper dimension of life. These writings are art forms in which poetry and story-telling combine to illuminate our humanity with a light which the darkness cannot overcome.

Something to think about.

Painting and sculpture are art forms representing truths that make noble human life. The Madonna and Child came originally from Egypt's Isis and Horus and gave expression to the female principle in human life. Mary and Jesus replaced the Egyptian figures to represent the love of God coming into life through the birth of a child, born in a manger. Christmas creches also point to the mystery of the particularity of the birth of the Christ child which in its own way, as In Hebraic thinking, expresses the mystery of God's involvement in every birth.

Paintings of the gifts of the Magi tell us that the Christmas message is not about one people but all people. Gentiles are represented at the manger to say to us that we Gentiles are there. Gentiles are welcomed; Gentiles are graced by the love of God. Paintings as well as stories speak in unique ways to the human condition. In spite of ourselves and our resistance to the familiar Christmas stories, they mean more to most of us than we are willing to acknowledge. Reinhold Niebuhr wrote that it is ". . . inevitable that the poetry of religion should be expressed in rational terms but something is always lost in the rationalization. Dogma is rationally petrified poetry which destroys part of the truth embodied in the tale." Trying to make rational or historical that which is essentially poetry undercuts the deepest truth found in an art form.

Something to think about.

Paradise is represented in great music. The universal language of music expresses in sounds the profound mystery of human life. Who has not felt a heart strangely warmed when hearing a piece of Christmas music? The religious community is blessed with some of the greatest music ever written inspired by Biblical stories. The quality of the music attests to the inspiration of God in both the story and the music. During the high religious holidays we discover a bit of paradise embedded in human life.

So once again we go to hear the angels sing whether in the form of choirs, solos, or in our own less than perfect voices. We hear music that we have heard before and are reminded that "love came down at Christmas, love all lovely, love divine," that "God so loved the world that He gave," that "peace on earth to humankind" is the thrust of the coming of Bethlehem's baby. Is there one whose soul is so dead that Christmas (or Hanukkah for that matter) has no message beyond the greed embodied in commercialism? Can we not discover some bit of Paradise in the various artistic expressions of the season?

Something to think about.

The story of the wise men from the East bearing gifts has more to it than a recording of something that happened long ago. This story goes far beyond an historical account. Pages ago we explored a deeper dimension than history in the story. Now consider another dimension. Think of gifts as a means of communicating the gift oriented nature of human life. Each of us has been gifted.

Christmas reminds us of the gift of creation: the skies above, the earth below and the water and atmosphere touching our planet are all utter gifts to us. We did not call them into being. Or, when at Christmas we are aware that "we are yet alive and see each other's face," we can be conscious of the gift of life. No one of us called the uniqueness of our selfhoods into being. And when we view again that Holy Family, we can be aware of both the families and the communities of which we are a part.

Christmas is filled with the fragments of paradise that reveal the often unacknowledged gifts of God to those with eyes to see and ears to hear. In all the busyness of the season, do not miss the bits of paradise showered into our souls.

Something to think about.

It's Christmas time! We feel it in the air. We sense it everywhere. In spite of the commercialism that affects all of us, something basic about the season filters through. Good will does penetrate this time of the year. We try to be more thoughtful of others. We contact many people whom we neglect most of the time. The season helps us to be aware of all those who have blessed our lives in times past.

But Christmas is more than worshiping the past. Christmas is very present calling for our relational responses to people now. The cards and gifts are all right as tokens of past relationships; but even more important are the possibilities of new experiences. The mangers are always present in life where new relationships can be born, where new revelations of God's love come to us through others. Nothing automatic here! We do our part by going here or there, by reaching out, by obeying the signs and signals. God's activity still comes to those who are awake and watchful. That is the deeper meaning of Christmas.

Something to think about.

Christmas speaks to humanity about the meaning of history. An historical figure came and lived among us. He went about doing good. He broke the barriers that separated the well and the sick, male and female, Jew and Gentile, the "righteous" and the "unrighteous." His followers experienced God in him. No wonder they gave him the "name above every name." No wonder stories emerged about his birth, his ministry, and his death that went beyond history to poetry and symbol and have become the inspiration for great music.

The nature of story is to take "never was" and make it into "always is." So with part of the Christmas stories that are paradigms for us today. "(Mary) gave birth to her first-born son and wrapped him in swaddling cloths, and laid him in a manger because there was no place for them in the inn." The Christ is always coming into life, room or not. Wherever there is human need, the Christ is there. "Inasmuch as you have done it to the least of these, you have done it unto me."

So be alert and watchful. In your mate, In your son or daughter, in your aged parent, in the stranger, in the hungry around the world, in the homeless and the destitute, the Christ is present to be born as reconciling, caring, and compassionate love. The Christ comes as grace (at times in the form of judgment). This coming is none other than reconception and rebirth which is nothing less than the second and multiple comings into our world.

Something to think about.

Christmas is a time for poetry, music, and story telling. The rational seems somewhat out of place. Reinhold Niebuhr observed: "Only poets can do justice to Christmas . . ." But his "only" is overstated. Music does speak to the inner self; and Christmas music, inspired by the birth stories, has touched numerous souls through the centuries. Story telling also probes past the rational to life's meaning. That's why stories by Dickens, Henry Van Dyke, 0. Henry, and many others touch responsive chords in us. No one asks whether the stories happened. Their truth is beyond facticity.

So I believe the Christmas story not because it is factual but because it is true, deeply and profoundly true. What is conveyed is that God has purposes which are relevant to humanity's journey. Behind the Christmas story is the mystery of life and the majesty of the divine which transcends human life. Any attempt to explain the stories, to make them factual, loses something of their profundity. Poetry, music, and storytelling are the appropriate media for conveying the message that God has entered human life to redeem it from meaninglessness.

Something to think about.

Where are the wise men? The Christmas story says that they came' from the east. Many still do. Those from India and Japan tell us to be more concerned about the economy and less about armaments. They reveal greater interest in public welfare than about corporate profits. They advocate sacrifice for the sake of the education of the young instead of capital gains advantages for the already wealthy.

Where are the wise men or womem from the west? They are not absent—just not heeded. Remember Bertrand Russell. Take heed of Norman Cousins' books, some of which are still in print. Pay attention to William Sloane Coffin. Read Rachel Carson. Give ear to Ralph Nader. Don't overlook the likes of Buckminster Fuller. And take seriously the works of Raymond Brown. And there are others, the wise people in the recent past; and present

The wise are still with us but so often neglected in our obsession with power, privilege, and position.

Something to think about.

The day after Christmas may find us in the doldrums. The gathering of families is about over. The special food and festive table have been replaced by left-overs. The giving and receiving of gifts has happened and we may wonder if it all was worth it. The Christmas sights are beginning to appear old and bedraggled.

The aftermath of the Christmas story in Matthew is like that. He brings us back to earth. After the birth and wise men, Herod threatens the newborn. The Holy Family flees to Egypt with all the realities of uncertainty, fear and apprehension. Nevertheless, the love of God is present. He is no string-puller, intervening in human affairs by disrupting the natural order. Instead God is the presence offering love, comfort, and sustaining grace which enabled people then, and enables us now, to live in faith, hope and love. This is the truth that remains after Christmas.

Something to think about.

Following the Christmas story is the word about Herod slaughtering the innocent children. The innocents are still being slaughtered: on the highways of our nation, in senseless shootings on our streets and in businesses, in terrorist bombings, in homes where handguns are too easily available, and in countless other ways.

What sort of world is this? What kind of God would allow the killing of the innocents? Look at the whole story. What happened to the innocents also happened to the one we call God's own son. He was killed. The word is not that God pulls strings to make things happen or to prevent them from happening. God is the caring and loving presence that suffers with us. We are with God and God with us in the work to perfect God's creation. That is the great drama of life. When innocent ones are lost in the process, we are brought together into a community of caring love. This is the best that we or God can do under the circumstances. To wish otherwise is to want immediately another world which is the most uncreative response to life.

Something to think about.

The Christmas stories linger. They are part of our lives. The Bethlehem stories of Jesus, for instance, are part of the "isness" and not the "wasness" of life. Bethlehem is a permanent deposit in the minds and hearts of followers of Jesus. No matter what happens to us personally or in our world, Bethlehem is still there and always will be. Bethlehem is still the place to look for tidings of comfort and joy. Bethlehem stands for the faith that the divine has entered human life.

That city of David remains as the symbol of our relationship to the eternal; the symbol that the universe is not indifferent to us; the symbol of a source of caring love available to all; a symbol of hope that remains in what is often a weary world. Bethlehem is still the place where we are fed the bread of life. History or not history, literalism or poetry, Bethlehem resides in the hearts of those who live by faith and not by sight. In the final analysis we live not by what we know but what we trust in. Bethlehem and Christmas say that this is eternal love.

Something to think about.

Christmas seems always to be a time of mixed emotions. Nostalgia is present for much of the older generation who remembered Christmases long ago and people no longer present. Excitement is part of the life of children (young and old) entranced by all the lights, music, and symbolism of the season. Loneliness is part of some lives who may have been alone on Christmas day. Yet everyone can be fed. Ministering angels are present to those who are sensitive to more than surface facts.

Angels are messengers with an energizing word. "Panis Angelicus," a spiritually probing song sung by Pavarotti during the season means "bread of angels."

Where are you fed? By a family member or friend? By a pet? By inner resources? By books or music? Angels are not ephemeral creatures with wings. They are the sources of nourishment for us found in usual and unusual places.

The Christmas story is peopled with angels. If you are not looking for an apparition or some other supernatural experience, you may find the angel near at hand, perhaps even "closer than breathing and nearer than hands and feet."

Something to think about.

When Christmas is over we move into another year. Most of us are not alone at Christmas. We are with family which told us that we are not forsaken. There are those who care for us, are concerned about us, and want to be with us on occasion.

This fact does not eliminate loneliness, however. Being human is an individualized experience. We are each wrapped up in a body of skin and remain throughout our lives separated from everyone else. At times we are aware of being isolated, apart from others. At such moments we can find sustenance in the awareness of the eternal Presence. The Christmas story offers us a loving and compassionate word giving us hope in humanity and confidence that we are not forsaken in whatever state we find ourselves. In fact, as the Indian poet Tagore has put it: "Every child comes with the message that God is not discouraged."

As we face the gate of the New Year, somewhat fearing what may be ahead of us and yearning for some light, we are urged:

Go out into the darkness and put your hand into the hand of God. That shall be to you better than a light and safer than a known way.

— Minnie Louise Haskins

Something to think about.

QUESTIONS FOR THOUGHT AND DISCUSSION

1. What is the meaning of Advent?

2. Nativity stories are pregnant with meanings beyond literalism. What are some of these deeper meanings?

3. Christmas stories have stimulated the arts. What in the arts have enriched the meaning for you?

4. What difference does Christmas make in your life?

CHAPTER 17

About After Christmas Into a New Year

When we celebrate a New Year, we know that the separation of one year from another is a human invention. Our calendar is not built into creation. Yet, the days, months, and years are a great help and convenience. With a New Year we begin anew. This is the wondrous part of life's endings and beginnings. Think about it.

How frustrating it would be if a day never ended and a week had no day of rest after which to begin again. In addition, the year coming to a close gives us the opportunity to assess our lives. The New Year, which is usually dignified by capital letters, comes to us with its clean slate. The future has no sins, mistakes or no "boo-boos,' as my grandchildren used to say. Forgetting what is behind (not always an easy task), we press on to the future as people who can embrace our lives as forgiven and accepted, warts and all. The word from the Book of Revelation, "Behold I make all things new." is especially true. We need not be the Lucys (Peanuts comic strip) who look out on a New Year's day and say that, nothing has changed. It has in the most profound sense. We can say by faith and in repentance that what has been is over and we have a new start, a clean slate. Thanks be to God.

Something to think about

"Time, like an ever rolling stream, bears all its sons (and daughters) away." So says the verse in a familiar hymn. In the first month of a new year we are often more aware of time than usual. We wake up in the mornings with the gift of time to be about the business of living. But we are all growing older. How do we deal with that reality?

We cannot keep from growing old on the outside but we can keep young on the inside. How? In community! One way to make friends with time is to stay friends with people of various ages. By ourselves, time becomes a threat. With others we find companionship in the midst of time and are made aware that we are not indispensable. The world and its future do not depend exclusively on us. Companionship across the age barriers helps to redeem the times and keeps us young inside.

When with the young, we are aware that the future rests more with them than with us of the older generation. To them we throw the torch and say with the poet: "Be yours to hold it high. If you break faith with us who die, we shall not rest . . ."

Something to think about.

Lent in the Church Year is preparation for the Holy Week that begins with Palm Sunday. How fickle we human beings are. The person we cheer one moment is booed the next. It happens at athletic events. So it was with Jesus. "Blessed is the One who comes in the name of the Lord!" This was followed later by "Crucify him! Crucify him!" When we are true to ourselves we know that we are there, that the story is about us.

Why is it that the people we love one moment, we hate the next? The sweetness of one minute is followed by the sourness of another? The experience of ecstasy is soon followed by misery? No simple answer, but one possibility is expectation. We expect people to act in certain ways. They don't always. We expect life to come to us in certain configurations. Sometimes but not regularly! We ex-pect to find constant satisfactions but we do not. Life's agenda is always being changed on us. The key is focus. Centered on our wants, we shall often be disappointed and distraught. Acceptance of and responding to the agenda given us is the challenge of life.

Jesus did not meet the expectations of many in his day. Many were expecting a warrior-king and Jesus came as a servant. Their expectations got in the way of recognizing what Jesus was about. Some cried: "Crucify him!" And his own disciples fled.

Something to think about.

Tuesday of Holy Week has been called the day of controversy. In the gospel story the enemies of Jesus confronted him and tried to trap him in conversation so that he would be discredited in the eyes of the people. How patient he was in the midst of controversy! He did not lose his cool, as we are prone to say. He gave the questioner the benefit of the doubt and treated the questions seriously. He did not prejudge the motives. As such he is in control of both himself and the situation.

Oh to be like that! I have lost my cool at time and missed the opportunity really to be in dialogue. Confronted by a disturbing idea or contrary opinion, we often become defensive and hostile. Such response is seldom productive. Hostility begets hostility and the end is separation. Jesus began by respecting his adversaries and responded honestly. I hear it: "Go thou and do likewise."

Something to think about.

Easter is the celebration of the emergence of life from death. Christians dare to affirm that this is God's perspective. Such a viewpoint seems to run counter to what our senses tell us. Nature appears to move from life to death. Each of us is deteriorating as we get older. The universe is running down. History is seemingly doomed to enter the abyss of nothingness. All ends in death.

Not so, says Easter. The disciples gathered, dejected over what had happened to their leader. But they changed. Something happened to convince them that the one who was dead still lived. What happened? We do not know for sure, but consider this: The disciples gathered in an upper room. Peter, perhaps, was the host. He was about to offer traditional Jewish prayers over bread and wine but remembered that Jesus had taken these elements a few days before and told them that this was his body and blood. Peter repeated that word. Then something happened. The story in John's Gospel is that the door being closed, Jesus appeared. I think they saw their Lord in one another. They were the new body.

What they thought was over was just the beginning. A new perspective was let loose in the world. What was that? The movement in God's activity is not from life to death but from death to life. In nature and history this perspective makes a world of difference. Centering on death leads to the negative spiral of depreciating all that we see. Focused on life, we see in every death new possibilities. What would you rather have – death or life? Choose life even in the midst of death.

Something to think about.

Spring is a wonderful season! Once again nature affirms that life overcomes death. The Song of Solomon (2:11-12) puts it this way:

> ". . . for lo, the winter is past,
> the rain is over and gone.
> The flowers appear on the earth,
> the time of singing has come,
> and the voice of the turtle dove
> is heard in our land."

Spring is an invigorating time: house cleaning, yard work, garden planting—all come into focus with the changing season. And the Easter season of the Church Year projects our attention on resurrection, life following death. Death is not the last word. We may be tempted at times to think that the movement is from life to death. Resurrection says No! The eyes of faith see death being overcome by life. Resurrection is a powerful symbol of new life and hope for the future. Don't you need that? I do.

Something to think about.

Thanksgiving is one of my favorite holidays. As a New Englander, the day has special meaning. Thanksgiving is a celebration that unites both our national and religious traditions. We tend to glorify this period in our history forgetting that there is a dark side of the story. Our relationship with Native Americans has not been a laudable aspect of our history. We oppressed and repressed the Indian nations unmercifully. Injustices still are part of our current life. Where have we tested nuclear weapons? On Native American lands without their consent!

Our religious heritage is not much better. The Pilgrims came over to escape a repressive society. The Church of England persecuted the Separatists. You would think that the Separatists (Pilgrims) would have learned a lesson. They did not but became a repressive society themselves. Roger Williams had to flee to the Rhode island area to escape persecution. Down through history Christians have been repressive. Roman Catholics and Protestants alike have been guilty. You would think that today such repression would be a thing of the past, but examine the Religious Right's agenda. Their plan is to take over our country and impose their view of biblical principles and ethics on the rest of society. Repression is the inevitable result of making absolute one's literature, doctrine and ethics.

Something to think about.

Some people are "into" history and some are not. I must admit that history has never been my favorite subject, but my vocation has pushed me into history time and again. In spite of myself, history has been teaching me something.

The study of history has the ability to expand our vision of the possibilities for human lives and cultures. History is always illustrating the limitations of cultures past and thus enabling us to see the limitations of our own values, assumptions, and beliefs. This is why a study of history has led students to question and raise doubts about their own culture and values and opened them to insights from others. History gives us the opportunity to weigh alternative ideas and beliefs.

During the Thanksgiving period, I find myself looking back at the Plymouth colony and seeing not only their struggles and sacrifices to gain religious freedom for themselves but their rigidity in beliefs and practices that led to their persecuting those who differed from them. So it has been with those who leave no room for understanding or appreciating ideas and practices other than their own.

Something to think about.

Gratitude is a positive state of being that we accent on Thanksgiving. Some families, following an old New England custom, place three to five kernels of corn at each dinner place. (This is a reminder of that first winter when the pilgrims, short of food, had to count out the kernels.) Then the host invites each one to express for each kernel something for which that one is thankful. A meaningful custom!

Being thankful is one thing, but living thankfully is something else. Giving thanks takes Thanksgiving a step farther. Thanksgiving is being grateful for the gift of life by contributing to the lives of others. Thanksgiving is so appreciating our talents and abilities that we see them as obligations to invest them in the common good. Thanksgiving is recognizing what people have done for us by doing things for others. Thanksgiving is being grateful for happiness by working to make others happy. Thanksgiving is offering thanksgiving to God for the beauties of the world by helping to make the world more beautiful. Thanksgiving is having gratitude for what has inspired us so that we try to be an inspiration to others. Thanksgiving is thanking God for our measure of health by the care and reverence we show our bodies. Thanksgiving is so being grateful for each new day that we do not use the time foolishly.

Thanksgiving is putting into practice Albert Schweitzer's philosophy: "In gratitude for your own good fortune you must render in return some sacrifice of your life for other life." (With gratitude to Wilferd A. Peterson for this idea.)

Something to think about.

Our moments and our days are made meaningful by the right words. What do we say to one another? Words that complain and protest? Words that express bitterness and hostility? Words that are always asking for something? Words that cut and hurt? Yes, each of us utters such words but seldom do we feel good afterwards.

I know two words which when uttered by me or to me always make me feel good inside. Thank you. Thank you for being here. Thank you for caring. Thank you for your helpfulness. Thank you for hearing me. Thank you for being you. Thank you, thank you. And we can say thank you when no one is present: thank you to that Mystery that has called us into being and sustains us in being. When we do we touch hidden springs within us. We were meant for thanksgiving. Whoever is without thanksgiving is indeed poverty stricken.

Something to think about.

Envy is the great barrier to thanksgiving. Each of us has enough reasons for thanksgiving, but we do not get around to being thankful because we spend so much time comparing our state to others'. Envy does come to us rather naturally because each of us is limited in specific ways. There are always others who appear to be stronger, more fortunate, and with greater blessings,

We are constantly being bombarded by the media with invitations, suggestions, and possibilities that are embodied in others but not in ourselves. We feel at times to be inadequate; and, in fact, we are. Envy is part of our humanity. We cannot banish envy by mere act of the will. Perhaps we can capture envy in some positive way to contribute to our lives and not demean them. What would that look like?

Envy can make us aware of what we lack and by that awareness lead us into reflection on what we are and what we want to be. Envy can help us set goals and prod us to measure up to our highest potentials. Could it be possible that we can be thankful for the measure of envy that does not immobilize us into a poor me attitude but energizes us into a more productive life? Could be.

Something to think about.

Many people bless us. Offering thanks is an appreciated and appropriate expression when we are blessed. But for many aspects of life there is no person to thank. Yet giving thanks is needed. Whom can we thank? Use whatever name you choose: God, Lord, Father/Mother, Eternal One, Allah, Being Itself. Or, as one atheist recorded honestly in his diary following his wife's death, "I thank (...) that I ever knew her."

So thank you for the night's sleep, for the morning coffee, for soap to wash, for a razor to shave, for clothes to wear, for breakfast. Thank you for the morning paper, for news on TV, for those who pick up the trash. Thank you for the birds that sing, for the squirrel in the tree, for the dogs on my walk, for the cat in my garage. Thank you for a day to live, colleagues to greet, students to teach, meetings to attend, a column to write. And thank you for my partner in life, the evening meal, the inspiring music, the cuddling before sleep, the quiet night, the stars and silence. Yes, thank you for time given me, a life to live, and resources for living it. Thank you for being there at the heart of life. Without your being, my thank you's would be senseless offerings to empty space in a meaningless void.

Something to think about.

QUESTIONS FOR THOUGHT AND DISCUSSION

1. The New Year may remind us of time. What does time mean to you?

2. Lent, Holy Week, and Easter offer Christians time to reflect on Jesus's life. What can these periods mean for your life?

3. What does the celebration of Thanksgiving recall in your mind?

4. Does the way you celebrate Thanksgiving give you the opportunity to evaluate the blessings of your life?

5. For what are your thankful?

CHAPTER 18

Miscellaneous

(a number of one and two page subjects)

There are no questions at the close of this chapter. Individuals can ponder the thoughts on the many subjects. Classes can discuss the subjects as they choose.

We all want to experience wholeness of body, mind, and spirit. But we cannot be whole without the experience of meaning, a sense of well-being, at the depth of our lives. What is human life anyway? "A tale told by an idiot, full of sound and fury and signifying nothing?" as proposed by one of Shakespeare's characters. Or, is it "the penalty you pay for the crime of being born?" according to a French existentialist. Or instead, is human life the most exciting experience in this whole universe? The greatest gift offered to any creature?

Life means something. Each of our lives is unique, special, unrepeatable. Each life has meaning and purpose; or does it? Perhaps you have never thought much about it. In that case, "where is the life you have lost in the living?" One of the problems in our fast-track society is that life is often lived on the shallow plane. Call it horizontal living. We seldom raise the depth questions. One anonymous poet put it this way:

> This is the age
> Of the half-read page,
> And the quick hash
> And the mad dash;
> The bright night
> With the nerves tight,
> The plane hop

161

And the brief stop.
The lamp tan
In a short span;
The big shot
In a good spot.
And the brain strain,
And the heart pain,
And the cat naps Till
the spring snaps; —
And the fun's done.

Something more than this is possible, which we shall explore in the next pages to give us—
Something to think about.

I have been a teacher, and I never cease to be amazed at what some students contribute in class and on papers.

Articles have been written on some of the humorous inanities, misconceptions, and misperceptions. I want to share one positive contribution.

In a class discussion on sexuality one semester, a young woman shared some advice she received from her mother. "First share your thoughts, then your emotions; then share your heart and only then share your body." What an enlightened perspective! This is so much better than the legalisms with which we often bombard our youth. What this says is that human beings are much more than bodies. If we jump too quickly into body sharing, we may never get in touch with the real person. We get hooked into the physical relationship and never really get to know the other.

When we share our thoughts, our emotions, and our hearts, then we get to know the other. This knowing is what justifies the physical relationship. The physical becomes the frosting on the cake and the cementing and stabilizing of the relationship. In this way the body expresses a oneness that is more than physical; it is spiritual. In the earlier sharing we have time to test whether or not our "spirits" are in right synchronization. Without such sharing we open ourselves to becoming enslaved to the physical and later disillusionment. We are, after all, more than physical creatures.

Something to think about.

I have a wishbone painted silver with a bow. Nana gave it to me over eighty years ago—an expression of love to a small grandson. We ate the turkey on a Thanksgiving Day. Since grandfather was a butcher, our turkey was large; twenty-eight pounds is what I remember. Nana dried the wishbone and presented it to me at Christmas.

That wishbone is about all I have left from those halcyon days. All gone except my brother and a cousin, and I have only limited contact with them. I cherish that wishbone. It reminds me of a love past. No one else can quite understand what it means to me. I want it with my body on that final journey because it can mean very little to anyone else. It represents a significant person, place and time in my childhood.

Why do I share this personal bit with you? I suspect that you have a remembrance or two stashed away. Every now and then you come across the item saved and you pause to remember someone, some place, another time. Hopefully you are blessed in the remembrance. What is true about me I dare to think is true of many of you out there.

Something to think about.

We marvel at the years granted to many today. An increasing number of people are reaching one hundred, and this increase is likely to continue. We celebrate old age when faculties are still sharp and relationships continue to be meaningful. Yet, I join St. Augustine to say: "It is no great thing to live long . . ., but it is a great thing to live well."[1]

What is it to live well? To enjoy the moments and the days. To refuse to be a malcontent whatever one's physical condition. To re-enjoy parts of one's life that were pleasant as blessed memory is called upon. To appreciate in thought old friendships with people no longer living. To remember special places where one experienced happiness so that one's heart tingles with the memory. But not to be satisfied just with memories, to enter the relationships at hand ready for new experiences, conversations, and sharing of time and energy.

Memories are precious. Hold on to them. Use them in quiet and lonely moments; but always be ready for the new. "This is the day the Lord has made. Let us rejoice and be glad in it." (Ps. 118:24)

Something to think about.

---

1. St. Augustine: Harmony of the Gospels, Sermon LXXVII.

Churches do many things but one thing is essential above all else: worship. Called a service of worship, the gathered communities of faith do more than serve themselves. They are also serving society by providing rituals that enact the memory and vision of what humanity is essentially. As John Westerhoff has written, church buildings are symbols of the home of the soul. The soul is nothing less than the essence of humanity that resides in each of us. No matter how successful a church may or may not be in its program life, if it continues to invite people to participate in its liturgies, it need not question its place, mission, or influence in the world.

We are living in a time when many are forsaking rituals for a fast pace of living, filling every moment with something to do or a place to go. In so doing we are losing the symbolic aspects of life — those pointers to the transcendent dimension. Without that dimension we can become a race of clever devils, a branch of the animal kingdom seeking for me and mine to survive at the expense of others. This is hardly humanity at its best. Churches keep alive another vision and this is their main function. All else is derivative.

Something to think about.

Human error plagues us all. Most of us do not like to admit our mistakes. The problem for most of us is accentuated for the absolutists who operate with the assumption that they have the truth. Absolutists see the evil in the world as external; it is out there in others. What's wrong are the liberals, the main-stream preachers, the atheists, the secular humanists and so on. To see the wrong out there is very exhilarating. We are off the hook; we are in. The danger is self-righteousness and pride.

Such a perspective is denied the Christian. Only as we see a need for our own conversion as well as the world's are we in harmony with Christianity at its best. From Hosea in the Hebrew Scriptures to Paul in Christians Scriptures, we find people who know that they are in the wrong and need the grace of God. Only in humility, knowing that we have not arrived at any final state, that our ideas and perceptions are limited, are we ready to receive the grace of God. That grace may come even through those with whom we disagree.

Something to think about.

Some of us at times spend much emotional energy worrying about our failures and weaknesses. When we falter in life, we act as though the error never should have happened, that all we do should be perfectly in order and correct in every way. How unrealistic can you get? No, I am not advocating that we go about making mistakes in reckless abandon. And we need to heed that word about being perfect as God is, even though that perfection will always elude us. But if we are not headed in that direction, we are focused toward the opposite. Imperfection is hardly a worthy goal.

Perfection is always ahead of us. In the process of living we learn more from our failures and weaknesses than from our successes and strengths. Be grateful for the learning that is constantly taking place as we stumble here and fall there. Just think, we might be perfect and then what would we have to look forward to?

Something to think about.

Who hasn't waited in a doctor's office? How do you wait? Fret? Constantly examine your watch? Wonder why you came early or even on time? Entertain thoughts critical of a system that cannot keep on a schedule?

Of course, you could have remembered to bring something along to read. Most reading in a doctor's office, I have noted, is old, dating back several months or even a year. But you forgot to bring something. Then meditate! Practice focusing on a thought or object. Probe various aspects of the subject. Let your mind wander. You may be surprised at what your mind can do when you let it loose. Fretfulness, anxiety, criticalness are all non-productive, non-creative ways of using extra time. You and I can do better than that and snatch a blessing from a serendipitous gift of time.

Incidentally, I wrote the first draft of this in a doctor's office.

Something to think about.

What is life all about? Some suggest that life is for pleasure. "Eat, drink and be merry for tomorrow we die." This is hedonism with no higher goal for human life than immediate satisfaction. The biblical perspective is quite different. History has a goal: the kingdom of God, the reign of God in human life. What is this but a kingdom of righteousness and peace where reconciliation is life's agenda. We have been reconciled to God; therefore, we are to be reconcilers.

To be reconcilers means growth in grace, in the ability to share in a world that is still becoming. This involves constant change as we become more like the nature of God who brought something out of nothing and sustains what is. At our best we bring new possibilities to life (the liberal spirit) and sustain all that is worth preserving (the conservative spirit). All of us are needed whatever our social and political persuasions. Do not disparage the conservatism or the liberalism of your neighbor. Both are needed for fullness of life.

Something to think about.

What is the purpose of life? If there is none, perhaps Shakespeare's word is correct: Life is a "tale told by an idiot, full of sound and fury and signifying nothing." Or, the existentialist may point to the truth with the word: "Life is the penalty you pay for the crime of being born." (Camus)

However, I resonate more with the affirmation in the Westminster catechism: "The chief end of man is to glorify God and enjoy Him forever." I was reminded of an account some time ago involving the mayor of Charlotte, North Carolina who was being criticized for her prayer breakfasts. In an interview she was questioned about her faith commitment. She responded: "If my life is for any purpose other than to glorify God, what can it be? In 100 years or ten years, who will ever know or care but God?"

I take comfort and find assurance with the conviction that in the providence of God, no deed is forgotten, no life is unknown, and no person is confined to oblivion

Something to think about.

Humanity has had a long fascination with life after death. A number of books have been written in recent years about after death experiences of those who "died" and were revived. Such near death accounts do not offer much to me. Perhaps I am too much of a skeptic about the bandwagon phenomenon in most of the accounts.

"After death" concerns are not very useful in this life and are, for the most part, socially unproductive I suspect that we are better off not knowing what is ahead for us. A Christian agnosticism is more suited to faithful living. Our energies are best used solving the problems in this life instead of trying to ascertain what is after death. The most exemplary religious people do not seem to be preoccupied with life to come. I cannot imagine that any of us would be better off from having advanced knowledge of what lies beyond the grave.

Embrace this life. Be responsible for the gift of life by living life to the fullest and trust that whatever comes is in the hands of a loving God. That should be enough for us.

Something to think about.

There is no human desire that was developed in us for no end. We hunger for food and there is food. We long for beauty and we find it. We look for companionship and it is available. We are eager to contribute something to life and we have work. We reach out for eternity, for a destiny past our own short lives, and, no matter how elusive, most of us believe it is there.

How strange that even base and corrupt qualities serve a purpose. We have at times an exaggerated sense of self-sufficiency which, when we come to the end of our tether, leads us to reach out in dependency. We even at times doubt and deny the reality of God, which can serve the ends of charity. Is it not so that when some need arises, we cannot with our doubts place this in God's hands? Doubting God, unsure of God, means that perhaps the only one to meet the need is myself. Strange how many things work together for good, even our doubts.

Something to think about.

Some of life's problems are unavoidable. How do you exercise some control over your children? What do you do when the income is not sufficient to take care of the expenses? How do you respond to the word that you need some surgery? How do you react when you see conduct at work that needs to be reported to some authority? The temptation is to try to avoid the problem, to procrastinate in making a decision, or to attempt to shift the responsibility to someone else. Usually we are not successful in these dodges, and the problem remains.

Somewhere I heard it said that when a Montana buffalo sees a storm coming, he walks into it. How did this creature learn that this is the quickest way to get through a storm? The best way to deal with a problem is head on without excuses or subterfuges. Perhaps this is what Jesus meant when he said to the invalid at the pool of Bethzatha, "Rise, take up your pallet, and walk."(John 5:1-6) In other words, face your situation head on and deal with it.

Something to think about.

In many minds doubt is a negative. We want to know, to have certainty; but we cannot. We are fallible creatures living constantly with uncertainties. In the Genesis story, Eve wanted certainty and tried to escape her creaturely state. Her reaching out represents a commendable trait compared to Adam who in dull fashion simply ate. Yet Eve's attempt to be more than human was doomed to failure. The human state is to live with uncertainty and to entertain doubts.

Certitudes in history and in our own culture have restricted thought, weakened or ended tolerance, and stifled the dialogue so important in a democratic society. Doubt leads to questioning and to new discoveries and insights. This is what troubles me about some religionists today who are unwilling to acknowledge doubt. One prominent figure in the Christian Right was interviewed and asked if he had any doubts. The response: "Not since I became a Christian." No wonder the lack of dialogue or respect for opinions other than those of his affiliates.

To know the one in whom you believe is not to have answers to all of life's questions. Faith is not certainty; doubt is its corollary. A modicum of doubt must accompany the mustard seed of faith to keep us humble, open to others, and less self-righteous.

Something to think about.

Environmental concerns fill the news these days. Polls tell us that 75% of our citizens consider themselves environmentalists. Considering oneself to be and doing something about the environment are two different things. The problem is that industrial and technological societies have misconstrued the role of humanity upon planet earth. Also, many religionists have misinterpreted the Genesis word about having dominion over the earth. We have taken that to mean using for our own ends without regard to what is happening to earth itself.

The word "dominion" is related to kingship and kingship is not ruling for one's own benefit. The Oriental king ruled for the benefit of his subjects. The welfare of others was his responsibility. Today we can extend that responsibility to include not just humans but the entire planet. We have been allowing nature to serve technology instead of technology to serve all of nature and not just the human part. The Spirit is moving us today to see that dominion is not over nature but for nature. If planet earth is to survive, the time has come to shift our focus from a selfish concern for our own species to the welfare of the planet as a whole.

The earth is a living organism and we are just a part, a thinking and creative part. We are here to serve the earth. This is what environmentalism is all about. At least this is my growing conviction and I offer this to you as—

Something both to think about and act on.

Why do we sleep? That is not a foolish question. Researchers have been trying to penetrate the mystery of sleep for years. Yet they cannot tell us why we sleep or what measurable changes occur as a result of sleeping. They do tell us that sleep is an active state with the brain functioning in a variety of stages.

How long do you sleep? Some people sleep too much. More people are groggy from too much sleep than too little. Have you tried sleeping less to see if you need all the sleep you are getting? The average person spends twenty years sleeping. That is significant enough to merit attention.

Sleep is also a symbol or metaphor for a quality of life. Sleep is used in the Bible to refer to insensitivity. Fullness of life is keeping awake to the world and what is going on. Too much sleep can adversely affect sensitivity, awareness, activity, and creative reflection. Paul said it: "Remember how critical the moment is. It is time for you to wake out of sleep, for deliverance is nearer to us now than it was when we first believed." (Rom. 13:11) So, watch that sleeping!

Something to think about.

To whom will you be listening today? Most of us like to talk; it is harder to listen. Some sage has said: "Even if you know what you are talking about, it may be wise now and then to keep silent." Good listeners are rare. Yet we all know that when someone has listened to us, we have felt good and, at times, have experienced a resolution of a problem in the process of expressing it.

Perhaps this is why the Creator and Sustainer of the universe is silent. We are the talkers that require a listener. When others listen to us, they give us the gift of their silence. When we do not have a listener, we can pray and express our needs, hopes and dreams. The response will either be silence or that "still, small voice" which can be translated "the sound of gentle stillness." What is that but a helpful, creative, and enabling silence.

So listen to someone today and perhaps along the way someone will listen to you.

Something to think about.

What do we do with virtues? You have your list and I have mine. Some may overlap but others may be in conflict. The virtue of a law to legislate against abortion, for instance, is in conflict with the virtue of free choice. Shall 51% decide for the 49%, or do the two live together in tension allowing truth to work itself out in the process?

One position claims absolute authority for its "privileged insight" and would deny by law the other's insight. Is this legitimate in a free society? I am willing to grant you your insight and may even entertain the notion that you may be "right," but I am unwilling for you to legislate that insight. Perhaps, just perhaps, your insight is faulty and in need of the correction that is most likely to come when contrary views exist with equal protection under the law.

Something to think about.

What is it to be normal? In popular thinking there are two kinds of people: normal and abnormal or normal and disabled. Press this matter a little bit and we discover that everyone has disabilities. We are not dealing with an either/or but a continuum which runs from slightly disabled to greatly disabled. If we internalize this fact, we may be enabled to relate to other people more understandingly.

Consider me as an example. Although I appear to be extremely healthy, I have my disabilities. One of them involves eyesight which means that I cannot see signs up ahead as soon as I used to. And I cannot see my golf ball land after I hit a drive. I also have chronic neck soreness when I turn my head, the result of a long ago whip-lash injury. I could go on. I look "normal" but I am a person with disabilities; and so are you.

We have no perfect persons. In Hebrew thinking, the gift offered to God and the priest who offers it must be "without blemish." All that meant is that the offering is the best that you have. And the priest was not perfect although he was not to have any obvious deformities. In Greek thinking, perfection did not accrue to people but only to works of art.

What does all this say? No one can claim to be perfect. Jesus threw out the holiness code with its exclusiveness. He did not say "Be perfect" as we understand that term. There is no such word or even concept in Aramaic or Hebrew. No one of us is or can be in the physical sense. Why then are people with disabilities today still subject to exclusion, bias, prejudice and discrimination? Perhaps it is because we want to feel better about ourselves and minimize our disabilities. How much better to recognize that we are all disabled and are called to be understanding and compassionate with one another.

Something to think about.

Do you enjoy what you are doing? A quote from Ecclesiastes says that it is God's gift to us that we should eat and drink and take pleasure in all our toil. James Barry has written, "Nothing is really work unless you would rather be doing something else." What would you rather be doing?

Sometimes we have to do menial chores simply because they have to be done. But if day by day a person is doing what he/she does not want to do and would rather be elsewhere, something is wrong. We are free moral agents, able to make decisions by virtue of the freedom God has given us. To be tied to work that is constantly unsatisfying and unproductive is to be a slave. We were created to be masters of our time and talents. Enjoy what you do today or change what you are doing.

Something to think about.

How personalities differ! Some people are like us and with them we feel comfortable. Others are quite different and we are not sure about them. How would we have reacted to Martin Luther? That depends. Some of us would likely have been uncomfortable with his energy drive. He was also known to be rough and boisterous. His language at times was quite earthly and not as refined as some of us prefer.

However we should be careful about dismissing people on the basis of surface factors. Some of God's most effective servants have been people we might have least expected to be so. Luther himself said of some criticism directed his way: "God uses coarse wedges for splitting coarse boards." That is a word for many of us as we consider our attitudes toward others.

Something to think about.

Don't you like to get invitations? I do. To get an invitation means that someone is thinking about you and wants you present at this or that event. We may not always respond affirmatively but it is good to be able to have an invitation.

Life consists of invitations and responses. Every morning we receive an invitation: "Get up and face a new day." We have to respond. We can say, "No, I don't want to," and cover our heads to close out the world. We come to a meal time and the invitation is, "Eat." Again, we can respond affirmatively or negatively. To say "no" too often can mean loss of weight and eventually health.

Every step forward in growth mentally and spiritually involves invitation and response. The invitation is, "Think, consider these new facts and adjust accordingly." When we do just that, growth occurs. When we refuse and draw into our shells, the shell of comfortableness with the tried and true, we stop growing.

At a deeper level, whenever a new and significant experience comes into our lives, we are invited to stop and reflect. "What does this mean?" "Why? How? What?" When we accept the invitation and weigh the event, the happening, the experience, we become more aware and sensitive to the spirit dimension of life.

Jesus was an activist. He went about doing good. But he coupled that activism with moments of reflection. He drew aside to pray, to struggle with events, to draw strength from friends. Life was a constant invitation to stop and reflect. His response enabled him to receive life with the inner resources needed to meet whatever came. So look for the invitations. One is coming to you right now.

Something to think about.

Epictetus, the Stoic philosopher-slave, urged: "Seek not that things which happen should happen as you wish; but wish the things that happen to be as they are, and you will have a tranquil flow of life." That is an insightful word. What it means to me is that if we wish something other than what is, we spend our lives if-onlying. If only this is and so, life would be good. If only I had such and such, I could live happily. This is to seek our own life and thereby lose it. But to give up our own life, what at any moment we want, and accept what is that we cannot change, we find our lives. We are able to take what is and use it for our own good, the good of others and the glory of God.

Something to think about.

Everyone needs a friend, someone with whom you do not have to be anything or do anything, with whom you can just be yourself. Jesus wept over the loss of a friend. The story of Lazarus tells us that Jesus had a friend who does not seem to be a disciple, just a friend. With Lazarus he did not have to be the "Messiah" or a teacher or a miracle worker. He did not have to play a role or put on a mask. With his friend he could just be himself. No wonder Jesus wept. Such friends are hard to come by. Sometimes such a friend is one's mate and this is a blessed gift. Sometimes that friend is outside the family and offers you the freedom to be yourself. This is an underserved, unmerited, friendship. When this happens we are aware of being smiled upon.

Jesus wept for his friend and wept for himself. Do you have such a friend? You are fortunate. Do you want one? I see only one possibility: be one. Give yourself to another in non-calculating love and you may discover in the process a friend.

Something to think about.

Do you know that song of a few years back that goes: "Try to remember a day in September when hearts were young and O so merry"? The tune is appealing and the words somewhat reflective. Sometimes I try to remember and all seems a fuzzy blur. I have vague recollections of other Septembers here and there and I know that I experienced the excitement of school beginning and the crisp fall season. But I thank God that I do not have to go back anywhere for the joy of life or the merry heart. The present offers excitement enough and relationships at hand are too significant to spend too much time reflecting on relationships past.

Perhaps this is what the psalmist meant in saying: "This is the day the Lord has made. Let us rejoice and be glad in it." (Ps. 118:24) I am and hope you are too.

Something to think about.

Just about everyone talks about peace but who is working for peace? One of our problems is the word itself. What does it mean? If we use the Hebrew concept of "shalom" to get the content of our word "peace," I believe that we can go far toward relieving the fuzziness in our thinking.

Shalom is the right relationship with all of creation. Behind shalom is the vision of the peaceable kingdom. This vision includes a harmonious relationship among all the creatures in God's creation. This certainly means humans living together in mutual concern and helpfulness and humans relating to the natural world in a non-exploitive manner. The vision is an ideal which judges present realities. Unless we take seriously the ideal, we shall be satisfied with less. This leads to apathy and unconcern for little else than our own welfare, with the "our" narrowly defined.

Such peace does not exist in our present world. Hunger threatens millions; human rights are ignored over much of the planet; the threat of hostilities with modern weaponry hangs heavy upon us; the pollution of our environment proceeds at an accelerating rate; various species of animal life are rapidly becoming extinct. When will all this stop? Only when a sufficient number of people become peacemakers!

Now there's the rub. We cannot be peacemakers until we become justice workers. There can be no peace without justice. What is justice? Nothing less than each one getting his/her rights by virtue of existence, having come into this world! Those rights involve life, liberty and the pursuit of happiness. But injustice abounds in Central America, Africa and Aisa, as well as among the hungry, the homeless, Native Americans, homosexuals, and women in our country.

Should the Church be involved in justice issues? This would inevitably project us into areas of controversy. "We should stick with spiritual concerns," so some assert. But this all depends how we define "Church." A narrow definition puts "Church" into the religious or spiritual sector of life, regarded as confined to devotional exercises: worship, prayer, Bible reading, hymn singing and the like. A broad definition sees the Church as mission to a world that God so loves as to be involved in it. If God is in everything and everything in God, we cannot afford to limit the spiritual to the religious aspects of life. The spirit dimension intersects life at every point.

Something to think about.

Each one of us has potential. No one has been left out. Whatever the physical abilities, the I.Q., the energy level – everyone has potential.

What is yours? Work for an answer and you discover purpose. Knowing what we can be and do leads us on. Our potential gives us a direction.

When we are on the way we find strength – the emerging power of our person. That power enables us to make our contribution to human life.

Each of us has potential. Each can discover what that is. Look at yourself. What can you do well, or at least better than some that you know? Be realistic about yourself and discover where you can make a contribution, indeed even make a difference.

Something to think about.

My attempt to overcome the negative of stereotyping liberals is an impossible task in our time. Many minds are rigidly set. Yet in hopes that some are still "listening," I shall continue.

Christian liberalism's stress lies upon the life and ministry of Jesus and the way in which his relational style and transcendent focus have emerged as the most complete and perfect expression of the moral and religious quest. The biblical records are read by the liberal in terms of the historical, cultural and religious context of the time. This is what progressive Christianity is all about.

The Bible is the primary text for a study of the life of Jesus and the response to him of those nearest the events of his life; but it is not a repository of absolute truths. The authority for Christians remains, in the liberal or progressive tradition, with a living Spirit that unites, empowers, and directs the community of faith. Some Christians want and claim more than that and, in so doing, isolate themselves from the major body of Christians. I regret the division caused by those who are so certain they have the truth and that the rest of us are in error.

Something to think about.

In a Freshman Seminar class one semester, I had the students write a journal page on finances. One shared this word: "When your outgo exceeds your income, your upkeep becomes your downfall." This is a word worth considering seriously when so many of us get overextended. We live in a consumer based economy. Many buy things they do not need, with money they do not have, because of advertizing they do not believe, to impress people they do not especially like. What a state!

Either you manage your finances or they will manage you. You decide! Some in our society who live at a subsistence level will not be helped with this word. (But most who read this book do not so live.) We all know, or, if we do not, we should, that one of the four main reasons for divorce is finances. We allow ourselves to get in debt over our heads, and we take out our frustration on our mates. No one, or couple, should be in such straits. Help is available through bank officers and other financial advisors. Our financial resources may never reach our expectations or desires but we can manage them if we would.

Something to think about.

Clapping with one hand is an impossibility. Clapping is an enthusiastic response to a presentation, and in the process one hand needs the other. Enlarging on this, one person needs another. We were not intended to be alone. Although we may cherish times of solitude, some space separation from others, being alone is only satisfying for a limited time. We were created to be in relationship. Community is the key to fullness of life.

Enthusiasm needs another or others. The Adam and Eve story in Genesis represents the truth (among many truths) that humanity is communal. An emotional high (or low) calls for sharing and communication. That drive to share experiences is the natural desire for community. So, as it is impossible to clap with one hand, it is likewise impossible to be enthusiastic (filled with God, the meaning of the word) apart from relationships with others. Reach out to others, build your community, share your life with another or others. You will be glad that you did.

Something to think about.

Pain is inevitable but suffering is optional. No life is lived without pain: a mother in childbirth, accidents, cuts and bruises, deterioration of the body, sickness and death — all involve a measure of pain. Pain also flows from disappointment, grief, failure, and frustration. This is psychological pain and the hurt is real.

Suffering, however, is that turning inward in self pity, self-depreciation, depression, gloom and doom, and the whole poor-me syndrome. Such responses are optional. No one programs us to suffer. We do this to ourselves. How, then, do we not suffer? Not suffering comes from a deep sense of security in spite of what may be happening to one's body or world. That security is most likely to come from a religious life, from a transcendent relationship. This is what enabled the Apostle Paul to say that he knew in whatever state to be content. In such a relationship we can embrace our pains, learn from them, and be grateful for the resources that enable us to endure the pains. What is this but the love of life, the gift of faith in that Power which is both beyond and within us.

Something to think about.

Extremists are generally wrong whether in art, politics, morals, or religion. Their anxiety over what is over-against them leads them to reject everything other than their own position. Inevitably the extremist throws out the good with the perceived bad. Extremists are easily led to a fanaticism for seemingly simple solutions to complex problems.

Something else needs to be said. An equal danger is found in being extreme about extremists. The trap is to suppose that extremists are wrong about everything because they are wrong about some things. This can lead to a blind rejection of legitimate concerns and perhaps helpful ideas about how to deal with problems. Extremists may be too narrow in their views but they do have passion. Extremists have helped to eliminate feudalism, the rule of kings, the absolute right of states, and will in time help to moderate national sovereignty (I think).

Extremists can also be helpful even when they are absolutely wrong. They cause us to think about what is wrong with the ills of society and to come out with better solutions. I am grateful for the extremists to the right, which is hard to admit. They serve a useful function. And if I am more related to the extremists to the left (which is hard for me to see about myself), I would hope this provides an opposite pole from which an Aristotelian "golden mean" can emerge.

Something to think about.

Who are the extremists? The list should include super-patriots for whom it is our nation right or wrong instead of our nation right the wrong. Super-patriots do not want to give up an iota of national sovereignty to an international body. Read the record of the Constitutional Convention and how the individual states had this same myopic vision! Extremists would block social progress by cutting social spending not recognizing that the stability of a nation is measured by what happens to the least of those in that society. Extremists advocate less government while tolerating big business and big labor. The two need big government to moderate competing interests and concerns. Extremists advocate abolishing the income tax when we are the least taxed of the industrialized countries. True, the income tax has become over-burdened with regulations and needs desperately to be simplified.

Government reforms are needed. Welfare also needs to be reformed to assure that people who can become contributing members of society are not locked into dependency status. And certainly government waste and excess programs need to be trimmed for government to be more efficient.

But watch the extremes. They give us the two poles in the middle of which may be some solutions. Beware of selling your soul or your advocacy position to one side or the other. Anger, frustration, and irritability can be the result. (And I am writing these words for myself.)

Something to think about.

How easy it is to get our minds set into unchangeable patterns. We get ideas; we adopt routines; we embrace perspectives; and we follow the past as though all were set in concrete. We reject the new, the variant, and the innovative as though the different is indecent. Do we not at times regard what is true as that which is familiar?

So it has been that whenever someone suggests a new image of God, a new approach to biblical study, a change in traditional words and phrases or new patterns of thought, someone is going to cry heresy, unorthodoxy or some other pejorative term. To some, abandoning the old and familiar is abandoning God. Could it not be that the old, adequate for one age, is not adequate for another? That all conceptions, images, and ideas are subject to change in this ever changing universe? The mind is alive and growing and so is the God who makes himself known (process theology).

Something to think about.

Multiculturalism is a word bandied about much in universities today. We in the West have pulled off a major coup in the history of humanity. Other cultures have seen themselves as self-sufficient, relegating others to the status of barbarians, unbelievers, foreign devils or other derogatory states. We have had a growing recognition that all cultures have their achievements: music, science and philosophy, art and literature, and customs that have enriched human life. The concern to study other cultures and learn from them is a creative departure from the past.

What is true about cultures is also true, I believe, about that part of culture we call religion. Both Judaism and Christianity have learned and borrowed much from other religions in times past. Aspects of Zoroastrianism and Roman, Greek, and Egyptian religions have found their way into the Judeo-Christian faith. A Christian triumphalism that today refuses to be in dialogue with others or to admit that any other religion has anything to teach us is as faulty as turning one's back on multiculturalism.

Like certainty, self-sufficiency leads to pride and pretension and is a parasitic cancer which will result, if not excised, in the destruction of the larger body and itself in the process. Life is too filled with human variety to define so narrowly one's scope of concern and interest.

Something to think about.

Never stop questioning! That is an adage that is an offense to many. The desire for certainty has led many to embrace absolutist positions in religion, politics, and ethics. The problems with such a stance is that no room is left for considering options or the sensitivities of other people. What remains is rigidity and intransigence.

How much better to question one's own convictions, to subject those convictions to constant scrutiny, to listen to the opposition giving attention to why people think differently. How can one help but be in awe in confronting the diversities of our time? Am I sure that I am right and others are wrong? Such pride precedes a fall.

Questions are a prelude to growth. I like Rainer Maria Rilke's word: "Be patient with all that is unresolved in your heart and learn to love the questions. Some day you may live into the answers."

Something to think about.

Reading is getting to be a lost art. This is what many are saying when they consider how much time is spent in front of the TV. Can the TV ever replace the value gained from reading? I do not think so. In reading we are forced to use our imaginations to visualize scenes, to "see" people, and to enter the world of the author. TV, for the most part, does everything for us.

Even more than this, reading is that act in which I submerge my "I" to another. I loan myself to an author who thinks, feels, suffers and acts in me. When I get my "I" back later, then I can be quite different. With a good book, my "I" can be enlarged, informed, stimulated, sensitized, and inspired. This can also happen in the worship service whenever the Christian community gathers to read and listen to its story. The written word remains as an indispensable tool to our humanity.

Something to think about.

Do you ever laugh at yourself? I do. Sometimes I laugh at myself when I suddenly become aware of how serious and intent I am about something that does not deserve such intensity. Sometimes I laugh when I catch myself in an obsessive act—like when I continue to look for something that I really don't need to find. I don't want to lose that ability to laugh at myself. I agree with Norman Cousins who wrote:

"Laughter is a form of internal jogging. It moves your internal organs around. It enhances respiration. It is an igniter of great expectations"

Life is indeed serious business and not to be taken lightly. Decisions should be made with adequate care and deliberation. Yet, life not punctuated with laughter soon becomes dull and drab, and seriousness can easily turn into depression. Let the laughter come. You need it.

Something to think about.

Education is much in the news these days. Each summer another group of students goes out into the world having graduated in May. Why did they seek a higher education? In '67 when they were asked why they were going to college, almost 93% said that it was to develop a meaningful philosophy of life. By '87 that figure had dropped to 39%. Are you going to college to become well-off financially? In '70, 39% said that was so. But in '87 that number rose to 76%. A more recent poll would probably accent the difference. Is this greater honesty or a tragic loss in understanding the purpose of education?

Classical education was to develop the civic self, the responsible person in society, who would make a positive contribution to the human enterprise. Something tragic has happened if the main purpose of education is just vocational training to increase one's income. Economic determinism is a sure route to the loss of humanity and the cultivation of an acquisitive society without the graces of sympathy, compassion, mercy and love.

In all our talk about education, how easy it is to forget that higher education has a more comprehensive purpose than merely getting a job.

Something to think about.

A general assumption is that Christians are supposed to be optimistic. Is that really so? One of my professors used to say that he was a provisional pessimist but an ultimate optimist. I can understand this position, but I do not necessarily agree with it, unless I define optimism as hope. I prefer to differentiate between them.

Optimism is the attitude that everything is going to work out the way I want it to. My wife and I are going to remain healthy, live to a ripe old age together, have no tragedies in our immediate family, live a quality life, and finally die a dignified death. The problem is that none of these may prove to be true. This is simply wishful thinking.

Hope, on the other hand, is not thus and so is going to be the case (optimism). Hope is in God. Hope means that no matter what happens, I will not be forsaken, I will be held by the right hand, and resources will be available to deal with any situation. This is a hope that will not disappoint us if we keep in the faith relationship.

I am not especially optimistic nor am I pessimistic. I live in hope.

How about you?

Something to think about.

Hope is one of the primary Christian virtues, but not the exclusive possession of Christians. Hope does not deny the tragic character of much of life. Hope is not built on the "whats" but on a Who. Since the Who is ultimate reality, being itself (to which we give the name God), we have a peace that the world cannot give nor can the world take away.

Vaclav Havel of Czechoslovakia addressed this subject in a speech some time ago. I can do no better than quote what is one of the best statements of hope that I have seen.

"I am not an optimist because I am not sure that everything ends well. Nor am I a pessimist because I am not sure that everything ends badly. I just carry hope in my heart. Hope is the feeling that life and work have meaning. You either have it or you don't, regardless of the state of the world around you. Life without hope is an empty, boring, and useless life. I cannot imagine that I could strive for something if I did not carry hope in me. I am thankful to God for this gift. It is as big a gift as life itself."

Now that is really something to think about.

Bibliography

Armstrong, Karen, *A History of God*, Alfred A. Knopf, New York, 1993.
——, *In the Beginning*, Alfred A. Knopf, New York, 1996.
Borg, Marcus J., *Meeting Jesus Again for the First Time*, HarperCollins, 1995.
——, *The God We Never Knew*, HarperCollins, 1998.
——, *The Heart of Christianity*, HarperCollins, 2003.
Bracken, Joseph A., *Christianity and Process Thought*, Templeton Foundation Press, Philadelphia, 2006.
Church, Forrest. Ed., *The Separation of Church and State*, Beacon Press, Boston, 2004.
Clayton, Philip, *Transforming Christian Theology*, Fortress Press, 2010.
Cobb, John B., Jr., *Christ in a Pluralistic Age*, Westminster, 1975.
——, *Grace and Responsibility*, Abingdon, 1995.
Dorrien, Gary, *The Making of American Liberal Theology*, 1900-1950. Westminster John Knox, Louisville, 2003.
Dyson, Freeman, *Disturbing the Universe*, Harper & Row, New York, 1979.
——, *Infinite in All Directions*, Harper & Row, New York, 1988.
Eck, Diana L., *Encountering God*, Beacon Press, Boston, 1993.
——, *A New Religious America*, Harper, San Francisco, 2001.
Eiseley, Loren, *The Immense Journey*, Random House, New York, 1957.
——, *The Unexpected Universe*, Harcourt, Brace, & World, Inc., New York, 1969.
——, *The Firmament of Time*, Atheneum, New York, 1970.
——, *The Invisible Pyramid*, Charles Scribner's Sons, N.Y., 1970.

————, *The Night Country*, Charles Scribner's Sons, N.Y., 1971.

————, *The Man Who Saw Through Time*, Charles Scribner's Sons, New York, 1973.

————, *The Star Thrower*, Times Books, N.Y., 1978.

————, *Darwin and the Mysterious Mr. X*, E.P. Dutton, New York, 1979.

Fox, Matthew, *Original Blessing*, Bear & Co., Sante Fe, 1984.

Godfrey, Laurie R., Ed., *Scientists Confront Creationism*, W.W. Norton. & Co., New York, 1983.

Haight, Roger, *Jesus, Symbol of God*, Orbis Books, Maryknoll, N.Y., 1996.

Kazantzakis, Nikos, *The Saviors of God*, Simon and Schuster, New York, 1969.

Kung, Hans, *On Being a Christian*, Doubleday, Garden City, New York, 1976.

Kushner, Harold, *To Life!*, Little Brown & Co., Boston, 1993.

Meyers, Robin R., *Saving Jesus From the Church*, Harper One, 2009.

Miller, Kenneth, R., *Finding Darwin's God*, Cliff Street Books, 1999.

Moyers, Bill, *Genesis, A Living Conversation*, Doubleday, New York, 1996.

Niebuhr, Reinhold, *Beyond Tragedy*, Charles Scribner's Sons, New York, 1948.

————, *Moral Man and Immoral Society*, Charles Scribner's Sons, New York, 1949.

Pagels, Elaine, *Beyond Belief*, Random House, 2003.

Ricker, George M., *The Faith Once Given*, Westminster, 1978, Revised and Republished, Eakin Press, 2003.

————, *What You Don't Have to Believe to Be a Christian*, SunbeltEakin, 2002.

————, *A New Look at the Old Commandments*, PenPoint Press (Eakin), 2005.

————, *Something To Think About*, PenPoint Press, 2007.

Robinson, J.A.T., *Honest to God*, Westminster, 1963.

Smith, Huston, Why *Religion Matters*, HarperSan Francisco, 2001.

Spong, John Shelby, *Resurrection: Myth or Reality?*, HarperCollins, 1995.

————, *Why Christianity Must Change or Die*, HarperCollins, 1998.

————, *Eternal Life: a New Vision*, Harper One, 2009.

Thomas, *The Gospel of Thomas*, Translation and Annotation by Stevan Davies, Skylight Paths, 2006.

Tillich, Paul, *The Shaking of the Foundations*, Charles Scribner's Sons, New York, 1950.

————, *The Eternal Now*, Charles Scribner's Sons, New York, 1963.

Weatherhead, Leslie, *The Christian Agnostic*, Abingdon. 1967.

About the Author

GEORGE M. RICKER, Pastor Emeritus of University United Methodist Church in Austin, Texas, has taught religion classes at Texas State University and at Austin Presbyterian Theological Seminary. For eleven years he has been leading seminars in the Continuing Education Department of the University of Texas. Dr. Ricker is the author of *The Faith Once Given*, published first by Westminster Press and republished in 2004 by PenPoint Press; *What You Don't Have to Believe to Be a Christian*, Eakin Press, 2002; *A New Look at the Old Commandments*, PenPoint Press, 2005, and *Something to Think About*, PenPoint Press, 2007. His books have been used in study groups and Sunday School classes over a wide area. He lectures and teaches in many churches in central Texas. He has been a newspaper columnist and a radio broadcaster of one minute spots some years ago. The author is married, has three grown children, six grandchildren, and one great-grandchild. He enjoys tennis and duplicate bridge and attends, with his wife Frances, cultural events in the Austin area.

www.ingramcontent.com/pod-product-compliance
Lightning Source LLC
Chambersburg PA
CBHW060047100426
42742CB00014B/2729